PENGUIN BO

THE INNOCENT ANT

After taking a degree in modern languages at Cambridge, Nigel Barley trained in anthropology at Oxford and gained a doctorate in the anthropology of the Anglo-Saxons. After a period of teaching at University College, London, he was appointed Visitor to the Slade School of Fine Art. In 1978 he embarked on two years' fieldwork in the Cameroons before joining the British Museum in 1981. This was his first experience of anthropological fieldwork – and very nearly his last. But he survived to write this witty and informative account of his attempts to understand and record the Dowayo society in which he lived. On its publication the *Daily Telegraph* wrote of Nigel Barley: 'He does for anthropology what Gerald Durrell did for animal-collecting.' *A Plague of Caterpillars* (Viking 1986, Penguin 1987) records Nigel Barley's second trip to the Dowayo people, which he embarked on in order to observe their circumcision ceremony, a major tribal event that takes place only every six or seven years. *Not a Hazardous Sport* (Penguin 1989) is the hilarious and touching account of his visit with the Tarajans of Sulawesi. *Native Land* (Viking 1989, Penguin 1990) is based on a six-part Channel 4 television series that he co-wrote and presented, and was first screened in summer 1989; it offers a fascinating account of many aspects of English life today. His first novel, *The Coast*, is also published by Penguin and his biography of Stamford Raffles is published by Viking and forthcoming in Penguin.

NIGEL BARLEY

THE INNOCENT ANTHROPOLOGIST

Notes from a Mud Hut

PENGUIN BOOKS

To Jeep

PENGUIN BOOKS

Published by the Penguin Group
Penguin Books Ltd, 27 Wrights Lane, London W8 5TZ, England
Penguin Books USA Inc., 375 Hudson Street, New York, New York 10014, USA
Penguin Books Australia Ltd, Ringwood, Victoria, Australia
Penguin Books Canada Ltd, 10 Alcorn Avenue, Toronto, Ontario, Canada M4V 3B2
Penguin Books (NZ) Ltd, 182–190 Wairau Road, Auckland 10, New Zealand

Penguin Books Ltd, Registered Offices: Harmondsworth, Middlesex, England

First published by British Museum Publications Ltd 1983
Published in Penguin Books 1986
5 7 9 10 8 6

Printed in England by Clays Ltd, St Ives plc
Typeset in Monophoto Times

Contents

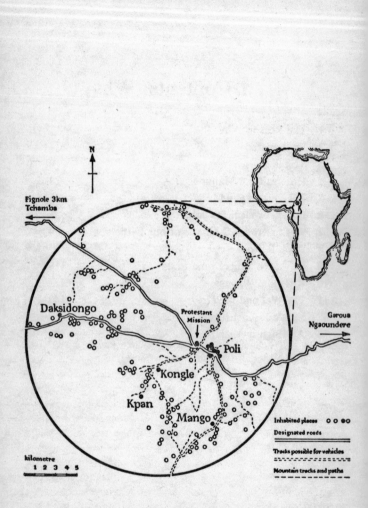

N

Fignole 3km
Tchamba

Daksidongo

Protestant
Mission

Poli

Garoua
Ngaoundere

Kongle

Kpan

Mango

Inhabited places   o o o ●●
Designated roads

Tracks possible for vehicles

Mountain tracks and paths

kilometre
1 2 3 4 5

1 The Reason Why

'Why not go on fieldwork then?' The question was posed by a colleague at the end of a somewhat bibulous review of the state of the art of anthropology, university teaching and academic life in general. The review had not been favourable. Like Mrs Hubbard we had taken stock and found the cupboard was bare.

My story was a familiar one. I had been raised in the institutions of higher education and drifted more by chance than design into teaching. University life in England is based upon a number of untenable assumptions. First, it is assumed that if you are a good student you will be good at research. If you are good at research, you will be good at teaching. If you are good at teaching, you will wish to go on fieldwork. None of these connections holds. Excellent students do appalling research. Superb academic performers, whose names are never out of the trade journals, provide lectures of such stultifying tedium that students vote with their feet and disappear like dew in the African sun. The profession is full of devoted fieldworkers, skins leathery from exposure to torrid climes, teeth permanently gritted from years of dealing with natives, who have little or nothing of interest to say in an academic discipline. The whole subject of fieldwork, we effete 'new anthropologists' with our doctorates based on library research had decided, had been made rather too much of. Of course, older teaching staff who had seen service in the days of empire and 'just sort of picked up anthropology in the line of business' had a vested interest in maintaining the cult of the god to whom they were high priests. They had damn well suffered the trials and privations of swamp and jungle and no young whippersnapper should take a short cut.

Whenever pressed in debate over some point of theory or metaphysics, they would shake their heads sadly, draw languidly on their pipes or stroke their beards and mutter something about 'real people' not fitting the clear abstractions of those who 'had never done fieldwork'. They evinced genuine pity for these deprived fellows but the matter was perfectly clear to them. They had been there, they had seen. There was nothing more to say.

After several years teaching the received orthodoxies in a department of anthropology of no particular academic distinction, the time was perhaps right for change. It was far from easy to determine whether doing fieldwork was one of the unpleasant tasks like national service that might quite properly be suffered in silence, or whether it was one of the 'perks' of the business that a man should feel grateful for. Colleagues' opinions were of no real help. Most had had plenty of time to enfold their experiences in a rosy glow of romantic adventure. The fact of past fieldwork is something of a licence to be a bore. One's friends and relatives are a trifle disappointed if every subject from doing the washing to treating the common cold is not larded with a sauce of ethnographic reminiscence. Old stories become old friends in themselves and soon nothing but the good times of fieldwork remain bar a few awkward islands of unreduced misery that cannot be forgotten or submerged in the general euphoria. For example, I had a colleague who claimed to have had the most marvellous time with agreeable, smiling natives bringing gifts of fruit and flowers by the basketful. But the inner chronology of the stay was provided by statements of the form, 'That happened after I got food poisoning' or 'I wasn't too steady on my feet at that time since I still had the festering boil under my toes'. One suspected that the whole business was rather like those cheery war reminiscences that make one regret, against all better knowledge, not having been alive at the time.

But perhaps there was something to be gained by the experience. Tutorials would never drag again. When faced with the obligation to talk about a subject on which naturally ignorant, I should be able to reach into my ragbag of ethnographic anecdotes, as my teachers had done in their day, and produce some long-winded story that would keep my pupils quiet for up to ten minutes. A whole range of techniques for squashing people also becomes available. The memory of one occasion, as ever, returns.

I was at a conference, dull even by normal standards, making polite conversation with several of my betters who included two very grim Australian ethnographers. As if by some prearranged sign, the others withdrew leaving me starkly exposed to the antipodean horrors. After several minutes of silence, I tentatively suggested a drink in the hope of breaking the ice. The female ethnographer gathered her face into a vile grimace. 'Nah!' she cried, mouth twisted with disgust, 'we've seen too much of it in the bush.' Fieldwork has the great benefit of making such phrases available; they are quite properly denied to lesser mortals.

It is the use of such turns of phrase, I suspect, that has conferred that valuable aura of eccentricity upon the really rather dull denizens of anthropology departments. Anthropologists have been very lucky in their public image. Sociologists, it is well known, are humourless, left-wing purveyors of nonsense or truisms. But anthropologists have sat at the feet of Hindu saints, they have viewed strange gods and filthy rites, they have boldly gone where no man has gone before. The reek of sanctity and divine irrelevance hangs about them. They are saints of the English church of eccentricity for its own sake. The chance of joining them was not to be lightly rejected.

To be fair, there was also the possibility to be considered – slight though it might be – that fieldwork would make some great contribution to human knowledge. On the face of it this seemed rather unlikely. Fact-gathering in itself has few charms. Anthropology is not short of facts but simply of anything intelligent to do with them. The notion of 'butterfly-collecting' is familiar within the discipline and serves to characterize the endeavours of many ethnographers and failed interpreters, who simply amass neat examples of curious customs arranged by area, or alphabetically, or by evolutionary order, whatever the current style may be.

Frankly, it seemed then, and seems now, that the justification for fieldwork, as for all academic endeavour, lies not in one's contribution to the collectivity but rather in some selfish development. Like monastic life, academic research is really all about the perfection of one's own soul. This may well serve some wider purpose but is not to be judged on those grounds alone. This view will doubtless not sit well either with conservative academics or those who see themselves as a revolutionary force. Both are afflicted by a dreadful piety, a preening self-importance that refuses to believe the world is not hanging on their every word.

For this reason, outrage was quite general within the discipline when Malinowski, the 'inventor' of fieldwork, was revealed as a rather human and flawed vessel in his diaries. Even he had been infuriated and bored by 'blacks', tormented by lust and isolation. It was widely felt that the diaries should have been suppressed, that they were a 'disservice to the subject', that they were gratuitously iconoclastic and would lead to all manner of disrespect for the elders.

This reveals a rather intolerable hypocrisy on the part of the purveyors of the art and should be remedied at every opportunity. It is with such thoughts in mind that I undertake the writing of this account of my own endeavours. There will be nothing new here for those who have undergone the same experience but I shall dwell precisely on those aspects that the normal ethnographic monograph punctuates out as 'not anthropology', 'irrelevant', 'unimportant'. In my professional work I have always been more attracted by the higher levels of abstraction and theoretical speculation since it is only by progress here that the overall possibility of interpretation moves closer. Keeping one's eyes firmly fixed on the ground is the surest way of ensuring an uninteresting and partial view. This book may, then, serve to redress the balance and show students and, it is hoped, nonanthropologists, how the finished monograph relates to the 'bleeding chunks' of raw reality on which it is based, and convey something of the feel of fieldwork to those who have not had that experience.

The idea of 'doing fieldwork' was now planted in my mind and the seed would grow as such things always do. 'Why should I want to do fieldwork?' I asked a colleague. He made an expansive gesture that I recognized as belonging to his lecturing repertoire. It was used on occasions where students asked questions like 'What is truth?' or 'How do you spell "cat"?' Enough had been said.

It is a polite fiction that anthropologists are consumed with a fire to live among one single people on the face of this planet whom they believe to be guardians of a secret of great relevance to the rest of the human race, and to suggest they work elsewhere is like suggesting they might have married anyone but their unique spiritual soul-mate. In my own case, my thesis had been written on Old English material in published and manuscript form. As I put it somewhat pretentiously then, I 'travelled in time, not space'. The phrase mollified my examiners, who nevertheless felt obliged to wag their fingers at me and warn me to work henceforth in more conventional geographic areas. I thus had no loyalties to any particular continent and, not having specialized at the undergraduate level, I was not repelled by any particular locale. Judging personally on the basis of completed work as the reflection of the people studied rather than as the image of those who had studied them, Africa seemed by far the dullest continent. After a great start with Evans-Pritchard the work tailed rapidly downhill into pseudo-sociology and descent systems as functioning wholes, rallying a little as it was dragged screaming into the consideration of 'difficult' topics such as prescriptive marriage and symbolism, but basically remaining true to its 'plain and sensible' persona. African anthropology must be one of the few areas where dull pedestrianism is advanced seriously as a claim to merit. South America looked fascinating but I knew from colleagues that working there was notoriously difficult politically; moreover, everyone seemed to be working in the shadow of Lévi-Strauss and the French anthropologists. Oceania would be a soft option in terms of conditions of life but somehow all Oceanic studies ended up looking much the same. Aborigines seemed to have the monopoly on fiendishly complex marriage systems. India would be a splendid location but to do anything sensible would require sitting down for five years to learn enough languages to make any contribution at all. The Far East? I would go away and look up what I could.

Such evaluations may, indeed, be qualified as superficial, but many of my contemporaries, and subsequently students, have operated precisely along these lines. After all, most research starts off with a vague apprehension of interest in a certain area of study and rare indeed is the man who knows what his thesis is about before he has written it.

I spent the next few months noting stories of government harassment in the Indonesian area interspersed with general news stories of atrocities and destruction all over Asia. In the end, I tended rather towards Portuguese Timor. I knew well enough that I was interested in cultural symbolism and belief systems rather than in politics or urban socialization and Timor seemed to show all sorts of interesting possibilities, with its various kingdoms and prescriptive alliance systems, where marriage with a certain kin-class was required. It seems to be a rule of thumb that neat symbolic systems often turn up most clearly where such phenomena occur. I was about to settle down and work out a project when the newspapers suddenly became full of stories of civil war, genocide and invasion. Whites apparently went in fear of their lives, starvation loomed on the horizon. The trip was off.

Rapid consultations with contacts in the trade suggested that I would do better to return to Africa where permission for research was less difficult and conditions more stable. I was directed towards the Bubis of Fernando Po. For those who have not come across Fernando Po, let me explain that it is an island off the coast of West Africa, a former Spanish colony and administered as part of Equatorial Guinea. I began to sniff around the literature. Everyone was highly uncomplimentary about Fernando Po and the Bubis. The British scorned it as a place 'where one is likely in late afternoon to encounter a sloppy Spanish official still in his pyjamas', and dwelt lovingly on the fetid heat and numerous diseases to which it offered sanctuary. Nineteenth-century German explorers dismissed the natives as degenerate. Mary Kingsley noted the island as affording the prospect of a large heap of coal. Richard Burton, it appeared, had amazed everyone by actually going there and surviving. All in all a depressing prospect. Luckily for me, as I thought at the time, the local dictator began a policy of massacring his opponents, using the term in a very loose sense. I could no longer go to Fernando Po.

At this point another of my colleagues helped by pointing my attention to a strangely neglected group of mountain pagans in North Cameroon. Thus I was introduced to the Dowayos who were to become 'my' people in love and hate from then on. Feeling a little like a ball in a pinball machine, I set off in quest of the Dowayos.

A search through the International African Institute index yielded a number of references by French colonial administrators plus one or two by passing travellers. Enough had been written to show that they were interesting: they had, for example, skull cults, circumcision, a whistle language, mummies and a reputation for being recalcitrant and savage. My colleague was able to give me the names of a missionary who had lived among them for years and of a couple of linguists who were working on the language, and to point the Dowayos out on a map. It seemed I was in business.

I began work at once, having now totally forgotten the problem of whether I wanted to go at all. The two obstacles were to get the money to go and the permission to conduct research.

Had I realized at the outset that it would take two years of constant effort to get both together at the same time, I might have returned to the problem of whether it was all worth while. But fortunately my ignorance stood me in good stead and I began to learn the art of grovelling for funds.

2 Be Prepared

I assumed the first time round that what was necessary was to show a grant-giving body why proposed research was interesting/new/important. Nothing could be further from the truth. When an inexperienced ethnographer pushes this aspect of his research, a grant-giving committee begins, perhaps on the basis of sound experience, to wonder how the research is standard/normal/a continuation of previous work. By stressing the vast theoretical implications of my little bit of research for the continued existence of anthropology, I was putting myself in the position of a man extolling the quality of the roast beef to a party of vegetarians. Everything I did made matters worse. In due time I received a letter telling me that the committee were concerned about the completion of the basic ethnography of the area, the brute collecting of facts. I rewrote my application in moronic detail. This time the committee were worried about the fact that I would be doing research on an unknown group. I rewrote; this time, they let it go. I received my funding. First hurdle down.

The problem of permission to conduct research now became paramount, since time and money were leaking away. I had written to the relevant ministry in Cameroon about a year before and been promised an answer in due course. I wrote again and was requested to submit detailed descriptions of the project. I did so. I waited. Finally, when I had all but given up hope, I received permission to apply for a visa and proceed to Yaounde, the capital. I confess with some embarrassment to old Africa hands that I naïvely assumed this to be the end of my contacts with bureaucracy. I suppose that, at that stage, I pictured the administration as a group of informal 'chaps' doing the small amount of administration necessary with good-natured common sense. In a country of seven million inhabitants, most of it would surely be done man-to-man in shirtsleeves as in the old British Empire days. The idiom would be one of solid understatement with everyone turning his hand to what needed to be done.

I might have learnt all sorts of lessons from the Cameroonian Embassy, but I did not. Instead I put all conclusions in abeyance, in best anthropological fashion, waiting until all the evidence was in. Having telephoned the Embassy to make sure they were open, I turned up with all relevant documents, feeling rather proud of my efficiency in having the two necessary passport photos. The Embassy was shut. Prolonged ringing raised a grudging voice that refused to speak anything but French and told me to come back tomorrow.

I returned the next day and managed to get as far as the hall Here I was informed that the relevant gentleman was absent and it was not known when he would return. I received the impression that asking for a visa was a strange and unusual thing. One useful fact, however, was gleaned: I could not apply for a visa without a valid return air ticket. I went to the airline office.

Air Cameroon regarded all customers as a confounded nuisance. I did not realize at that time that this was the way all government monopolies are run in Cameroon and put it down to language difficulties. They were suspicious of cheques, cash was inconvenient. I ended up paying for my ticket in French travellers' cheques. What other people do I cannot imagine. (One sound rule for the beginner: always deal with exotic airlines through a British travel agent. They will take payment in normal forms of currency.) While there, I inquired about trains between Yaounde and N'gaoundere, my next stop up country. I was sternly informed that this was an airline office, not a railway office, but it so happened that there was an air-conditioned train between the two. The journey took about three hours.

Flushed with triumph and armed with my ticket, I returned to the Embassy. The gentleman was still not back but I would be permitted to fill in a form in triplicate. I did so and was surprised to note that the top copy which I had laboriously completed was thrown away. I waited about an hour. Nothing happened. Meanwhile various people were drifting in and out, mostly speaking French. It is perhaps necessary to point out that

Cameroon was an old German colony taken over by the British and French during the First World War and subsequently given independence as a federal republic, later replaced by a unified republic. Although Cameroon is theoretically bilingual in French and English, it is a bold man who hopes to get far on English alone. Eventually, a huge African woman entered and I was the subject of a long conversation in a language unknown to me. I suspect now that it was English. If anyone approaches you in old British territory speaking a totally unintelligible tongue of which even the basic sounds are quite unfamiliar, it is probably English. I was led into another office where numerous volumes were ranged around the walls. I noted with interest that these contained the photographs and details of prohibited persons. It is still astonishing to me that it is possible for such a young country to have prohibited so many people. Having sought me in vain for some considerable time, the woman lay aside the volumes with what appeared to be a deep sense of disappointment. The next problem lay in my having produced two passport photographs which were joined together. They should have been separate and I was rebuked for presenting them in this condition. There began a protracted search for the scissors. Many people were involved in this, furniture was moved, the volumes of prohibited persons were shaken. Trying to show willing, I looked half-heartedly on the floor. Again I was rebuked. This was an embassy and I was to touch and look at nothing. Finally, the scissors were traced to a man in the basement who, it appeared, was not authorized to possess them. This was explained at great length. We were all required to show our outrage. The next problem was whether the visa should be paid for or not. In my innocence I gladly offered to pay for it, not realizing that this was a major issue. The head of the section would have to decide. Back to the waiting room, where finally another Cameroonian appeared who perused my documents with great attention and required me to explain myself yet again, looking the whole time extremely suspicious of my motives. The basic difficulty here, as in other areas, is explaining why the British government should find it worth while to pay its young people fairly large sums of money to go off to desolate parts of the world purportedly to study peoples who are locally notorious for their ignorance and backwardness. How could anyone make money out of such studies? Clearly some sort of hidden purpose is involved. Spying, mineral prospecting or smuggling must be the real motive. The only hope is to pass oneself off as a harmless idiot who knows no better. I succeeded in this. Finally I was given my visa, a huge rubber-stamped confection with what was clearly a heavily Africanized version of Marianne, the French revolutionary heroine. As I left, I felt strangely tired with a lingering sense of humiliation and disbelief. It was a feeling I was to grow to know well.

I now had something like a week to put my affairs in order and complete my arrangements. Vaccinations had played quite a large role in my life for some months and there remained only a final yellow fever shot before I was fully proofed. Unfortunately, this gave me a fever and vomiting attacks that rather diminished my enjoyment of farewells. I was issued with an intimidating box of drugs and a list of the symptoms they would cure, almost all of which I already had from the inoculations.

It was the moment for final words of advice. My immediate family, who were entirely innocent of anthropological expertise, knew only that I was mad enough to go to savage lands where I would live in the jungle, constantly menaced by lions and snakes, and might be lucky enough to escape the cooking pot. It came as some comfort to me when I was about to leave Dowayoland that the chief of my village said that he would gladly accompany me back to my English village but that he feared a country where it was always cold, where there were savage beasts like the European dogs at the mission and where it was known there were cannibals.

A book should doubtless be compiled of 'sayings to young ethnographers about to go into the field'. It is rumoured that the eminent anthropologist Evans-Pritchard would simply tell his protégés, 'Get yourself a decent hamper from Fortnum and Mason's and keep away from the native women.' Another West Africanist would reveal that the secret of successful fieldwork lay in the possession of a good string vest. In my own case I was told to complete my will (which I did), to take nail varnish for the local dandies (which I didn't) and to buy myself a good penknife (which broke). A lady anthropologist revealed to me the address of a London shop where I could buy shorts with locust-proof pocket-flaps. I felt these to be an unnecessary luxury.

The ethnographer is faced with a basic decision at the outset if he needs a vehicle. Either he can buy one here, fill it with all the goods he will need to survive and ship it out, or he can arrive unencumbered at his destination and buy what he needs from scratch. The advantage of the former method lies in cheapness and the certainty of finding what you want. Its disadvantage lies simply in the frustration of the extra contact with customs officials and other bureaucrats who will blandly impound it, charge duty on it, stand it in the monsoon till it rots, allow it to be rifled, insist on minute certified lists in quadruplicate, countersigned and stamped by other officials hundreds of miles away and otherwise gleefully harass and persecute the newcomer. Many of these difficulties will magically melt away in the face of a well-placed bribe, but the calculation of the appropriate sum and the point at which the bribe should be offered requires a fineness of touch that the newcomer will lack. He may well end up in serious trouble if he attempts this proceeding incautiously.

The difficulty of the second method, of simply arriving and buying what is necessary, is that it is extremely expensive. Cars cost at least double what they do over here and choice is very limited. The newcomer, unless he is very lucky, is unlikely to strike a good bargain.

In my innocence, I opted for the second alternative, partly because I had no time to prepare myself lavishly and was eager to be off.

3 To the Hills

As the plane landed on the darkened airfield at Duala a unique smell invaded the cabin. It was musky and sultry, aromatic and coarse – the smell of West Africa. Warm rain was falling; it felt like blood trickling down our sweaty faces as we hiked across the tarmac. Inside the airport was the most amazing chaos I have ever witnessed. Crowds of Europeans were huddled in desperate groups or screaming at Africans. Africans were screaming at Africans. A lone Arab was floating disconsolately from one desk to another. In front of each was the mad, jostling throng I recognized as a French queue. Here I had my second lesson in Cameroonian bureaucracy. It seemed that we had to collect three pieces of paper relating to our visas, health certificates and immigration arrangements. Numerous forms had to be filled in. There was a heavy trade in ballpoint pens. When the French had elbowed their way through to have the privilege of waiting in the rain for their luggage, the rest of us were attended to. Several of us made the mistake of being unable to supply exact addresses to which we were going and the names of business contacts. A large official sat at his desk reading the newspaper and ignoring us. Having established to his satisfaction our relative hierarchy, he interviewed us with an air of one not to be trifled with. Seeing the way things were going, I relented and supplied a wholly fictitious address, which was the recourse adopted by several others. In future I was always studiously precise in filling in all forms which were doubtless eaten by termites or thrown away unread. We all went back round the three desks again and through customs, where a drama was being enacted. A Frenchman's luggage had been opened and found to contain certain aromatic substances. In vain the man claimed that these were herbs to cook the sauces of French cuisine. The official was convinced he had captured a

19

major trader in marijuana, even though it was common knowledge that a trade existed growing it *inside* Cameroon and smuggling it *out*. The French jostlers were back in operation and seemed to be doing quite well until the huge form of an immaculate African who had got on the first-class section at Nice sailed through. With a click of his gold-adorned fingers he indicated his luggage, which was promptly seized by porters. Luckily for me, my own luggage impeded the removal of his and so I was waved through and out into Africa.

First impressions count for a lot. The man whose knees are not brown will be marked down by all manner of people. At all events, my camera case was promptly seized by what I took to be an enthusiastic porter. I revised my ideas when he swiftly made off into the distance. I set off in pursuit, using all manner of phrases uncommon in everyday speech. 'Au secours! Au voleur!' I cried. Fortunately, he was delayed by traffic, I caught up, and we began to struggle. It ended with a swift blow that laid open the side of my face and the case was abandoned to me. A solicitous taxi driver took me to my hotel for only five times the normal fare.

The next day I tore myself away from the charms of Duala and flew on to the capital without incident, noting that I had adopted the loud, hostile manner of the other passengers towards porters and taxi drivers. In Yaounde I suffered a long bout of bureaucracy; as it took about three weeks to have my documents processed there was nothing to do but play tourist.

My first impression of the city was that it had few charms. It is unpleasantly dusty in the dry season, a vast morass in the wet season. Its main monuments have all the appeal of motorway café architecture. Collapsed gratings in the pavements offer the unwary visitor a direct route to the town sewers. Newcomers seldom survive long without wrenching at least one limb. The life of expatriates centres around two or three cafés where they sit in deep boredom, staring at the passing yellow cabs and fighting off the attentions of souvenir sellers. These are gentlemen of the greatest charm who have learnt that white men will buy absolutely anything as long as it is overpriced. They offer for sale a blend of perfectly acceptable carvings and absolute rubbish as 'genuine antiques'. The whole trade is practised with something of the air of a game. Asked prices are something like twenty times what is reasonable. Should a client protest that he is being robbed, they giggle and agree, cutting their price to five times the going rate. Many enjoy something like a client/patron relationship with jaded Europeans, fully aware that the more outrageous their lies the greater will be the amusement they cause.

The saddest cases are the diplomats who seem to pursue a policy of minimal contact with the locals, fleeing from locked office to locked compound via the café. For reasons that will become apparent later, I occasioned the British community some inconvenience.

Far more interesting were the young French community of *coopérants*, people doing foreign service as an alternative to national service in the army. They had somehow managed to set up a replica of provincial French social life incorporating factors such as barbecues, motor rallies and parties with minimal regard to the fact that they were in West Africa. I rapidly established links with one ménage, one girl and two boys who were variously engaged in professional teaching and later proved invaluable. Unlike the diplomatic community, they actually left the capital and had information about the state of roads, the vehicle market, etc., and spoke to Africans who were not their servants. It came as a great surprise to me after the officials with whom I had to deal, how extremely friendly and pleasant the people were; I had by no means expected this. After the political resentments of West Indians and Indians I had known in England, it struck me as ridiculous that it should be in Africa that people of different races should be able to meet on easy, uncomplicated terms. Of course it turned out not to be quite as simple as that. Relations between Europeans and Africans are complicated by all kinds of factors. Often the Africans concerned have learnt to conform so well that they are little other than black Frenchmen. On the other hand, Europeans resident in Africa tend to be rather weird people. Their conspicuous ordinariness is perhaps the reason the diplomatic community fare so badly; madmen – and I met several of them – fare very well despite the havoc they leave behind them.

As an Englishman I was perhaps unreasonably impressed by

the fact that complete strangers would greet me and smile at me in the street, apparently without ulterior motive.

Time was passing and African cities are by no means cheap; Yaounde is classed as one of the most expensive places on earth for a foreigner. While I was living in no great style, money was going fast and I simply had to get out; I would have to make a scene. Steeling my nerve, I went to the Bureau of Immigration. Behind the desk sat the supercilious inspector I had dealt with on previous visits. He looked up from the documents he was reading and began an intricate process involving a cigarette and lighter, ignoring my greeting, and threw my passport on the desk. Instead of the two years I had asked for, I had been mysteriously given nine months in the country. Thankful for small mercies, I left.

It was at this point that I made two blunders that reveal how very little I knew about the world I was moving in. First, I went to the post office to send a telegram to N'gaoundere, my next staging post up the railway line, warning them of my imminent arrival. It got there a fortnight later, which was considered about average by old hands. It also acquainted me with a very odd Australian who, despairing of arrogant officials and locals who had learnt their jostling from the French, was reduced to standing in the middle of the floor shouting to everybody's surprise, 'I've understood. I'm the wrong bleedin' colour in' I?' He thereupon declared in good round terms that he never intended to write to his mother again from Cameroonian territory. Luckily, I was able to sell him one of my own stamps at which point he exploded in maudlin Commonwealth affection and insisted I take beer with him. After several of these he revealed that he had been travelling for more than two years and never spent more than fifty pence a day. I was suitably impressed until he took his leave without paying for the beer.

It was then I made my most serious error so far. Hitherto, I had kept the major part of my research grant in the form of a certified international cheque which I carried on me at all times. It seemed to me prudent to deposit this in a bank, which only took me about an hour of the jostling and arrogance treatment. I was blandly assured by a plausible young man that a cheque book would be sent to me at N'gaoundere within twenty-four hours and that I would thus be able to draw on the account as necessary. Incredibly, I believed him. In fact it took some five months to gain access to the money I had so lightly deposited. However, at the time it seemed a victory for reason in view of the many stories of crime circulating in ever more horrific versions among the white community. Many of the men have adopted the fashion of carrying small handbags, after the effete Continental manner, in which to keep the documents they are obliged to carry. It appears that gangs of huge African women roam the streets after dark snatching the purses of lone males, beating up those bold enough to resist. This is quite feasible. Africa is the home of the most astonishing physiques, both male and female, the result of lives of continuous hard physical labour and a diet low in protein. A willowy Westerner feels initially dwarfed by the pectoral developments of Southern Cameroonians.

It was with a certain sense of relief that I checked out of the hotel, mentally saying goodbye to the piped African guitar music that raged night and day, and running the gauntlet of the whores for the last time. These ladies are perhaps the least subtle members of their trade I have ever seen. A perfectly accepted mode of approach is to walk straight up to the intended male and simply grasp him between the legs in a vice-like grip; one should always avoid being closeted in the lift in such circumstances.

Soon afterwards I was safely at the station, becoming increasingly sceptical about the delights of the air-conditioned train described to me by the airlines girl in London. It consisted of First World War rolling stock, hailing by some mysterious process from Italy. It was lavishly embellished with exhortations in Italian about what to do and not to do with the water supply and toilet facilities. Problems of translation had been solved at a stroke by simply discontinuing them.

A little more jostling sufficed to buy a ticket, with about the same amount of form filling as one needs to buy life insurance.

Travelling in West Africa seems to have much in common with travel by stage in early Westerns. There is a fairly standard cast. It seems much the same whether one is travelling by train or bush-taxi; the latter plays a major role in getting about inside the country. Bush-taxis are big Toyota or Saviem vans built to accommodate from twelve to twenty persons into which the proprietors seek to introduce between thirty and fifty. Should the vehicle give the false impression of bursting at the seams, a popular expedient is to drive off at speed and apply the brakes, which always makes room for one or two more at the back. It seems to be required that each vehicle shall contain a couple of army corporals or lieutenants. Gendarmes normally find themselves the best seats, beside the driver, and blandly refuse to pay for them. A couple of southern schoolteachers resentful at being sent to the Muslim North are standard. With but little prompting, they entertain the company with tales of their sufferings in that benighted area, denouncing the lack of entrepreneurial spirit, the savagery of the pagan inhabitants, the inedibility of the food. Then there will be a pagan woman in blue plastic shoes suckling a child, an operation that seems to involve most of the women full time. A couple of gaunt Muslims from the semi-desert of the North, swathed in Arab robes and clutching prayer mats and kettles of water, complete the assembly.

So it was with the train. A technological development much appreciated by the locals is the cassette radio, so that a man may record a wavering cacophony broadcast through a thick hiss and crackle of atmospherics and play it back in public at high volume over and over again. There is always a competition between northern Muslims and southern Christians to establish prior rights to airspace. Winning this contest gives one the exclusive right to play one's cassette regardless of the hour and determines whether the theme shall be the interminable tuneless West African pop of Nigerian pijin ('O me mammy I don' forget you') or indigenous products ('Je suis un enfant de Douala olé') or the raucous wailing of Arab-style confections. Stopping for even a moment is interpreted as allowing the opposition its chance and is therefore discouraged. The principal difference between those areas of a city populated by local bureaucrats or foreign envoys is that of noise level. Africans seem genuinely perplexed by the Westerner's predilection for creeping around in silence when presumably he could afford enough batteries to have his radio playing day and night.

Another basic difference between Christian and Muslim is that the Christian males urinate standing up and are thus quite able to reach the sink in the washroom for that purpose, whereas Muslims urinate squatting, a process effected with dreadful risk by spreading out their robes to a capacious tent and half leaning out of the open door of the moving carriage.

On this particular trip I sat opposite a German agriculturalist heading north for his second term of duty. He was, he revealed, in charge of a project to encourage the cultivation of cotton for export. Cotton is sold through a government monopoly and earns much-needed foreign exchange, so its production is heavily supported by central government. Had he been successful? Wildly so; in fact the people had spent so much time growing cotton that they had grown no food, prices had rocketed and a famine had only been averted by the intervention of the church relief projects. Strangely, he seemed in no way depressed by this outcome, taking it rather as a sign that cotton had come to stay.

During my time in Cameroon I met many such specialists, some of whom reproached me bitterly for being a 'parasite on African culture'. They had come to share knowledge, to change peoples' lives. I was only there to observe and might, by my interest, encourage pagan superstition and backwardness. Sometimes, in the silent watches of the night, I too wondered about that, just as in England I had wondered about the point of an academic life. However, when it came to the crunch they seemed to accomplish very little. For every problem they solved they created two more. I rather felt that it was people who claimed to be the sole possessors of the truth who should be ill at ease for the disruption they caused in others' lives. At least one can say of the anthropologist that he is a harmless drudge, it being one of the professed ethics of the trade to interfere directly as little as possible in what one observes.

Such thoughts come to the fieldworker as he eats interminable bananas on a railway train. The journey, I'd been assured, would last three hours; in fact it took seventeen hours, but gradually the temperature dropped as we climbed the plateau towards the city of N'gaoundere. Night fell suddenly and the lights failed in the train. We sat in the gloom, eating bananas, talking broken German and watching the scrubby bush fade into blackness.

Finally, when I'd begun to feel that I'd spend the rest of my life on this train, we arrived at N'gaoundere.

There was an immediate sense of alienation, much greater than in the South. N'gaoundere is regarded as the frontier between North and South, popular with Whites for its cool climate and rail link with the capital. Although changing under the impact of the railway, it still maintains large areas of traditional thatched compounds.

Further south, these have been displaced totally by a passion for corrugated iron or aluminium sheeting, unbearably hot in the sun and acting as a vast radiator which ensures that night becomes as hot as day. These corrugated shanties contribute greatly to the ugliness of African cities to a Westerner's eyes. This is partly sheer ethnocentrism; while thatched huts are 'picturesque and rustic', corrugated huts are 'slums'. N'gaoundere, however, was less immediately offensive than most African towns. In the dark, with hundreds of cooking fires glowing, it looked like a Westerner's view of Africa. In the daylight one sees the piles of rotting rubbish through which the gilded youth picks its way on mopeds adorned with plastic flowers.

But for the moment, the German and I were totally absorbed in bargaining with a taxi driver. Whereas I would probably have accepted my historical role as someone to be robbed, the German devoted himself to haggling with the ferocity and apparent deep contempt for all taxi drivers that I came to note as the mark of a man who really knew his way around. The result was that we were delivered to the Catholic mission with minimum delay, at reasonable cost, and received warmly by the priests, whom he knew well.

There is a widespread impression that missionaries have taken upon themselves the mantle of medieval hospitality to travellers. Some do, indeed, provide lodging but this is more likely to be for their own personnel flitting between conferences than for vapid wanderers. They have suffered greatly from penniless hitchhikers who expect to be able to live off the fat of Africa as easily as they do in Europe. Under their onslaught, hospitality has necessarily been curtailed; otherwise missions would find themselves exclusively in the hotel business.

But I was eager to move on to the Protestant mission where I believed myself to be expected. With delays in documentation, I was now two months into my fieldwork time and had not even seen a Dowayo. I had a nagging fear they might not exist, the word 'Dowayo' being a native term for 'no one' that had been dutifully noted in answer to some district officer's question. 'Who lives over there?' I inquired politely at the Catholic mission. Yes, it seemed the Dowayos did exist. Fortunately the Catholics had had very little to do with them, they were terrible people. At the school the Fathers ran they were always the very worst pupils. Why was I interested in working with Dowayos? The reason for their mode of life was simple: they were ignorant.

4 Honi soit qui Malinowski

Young anthropologists know all about missionaries before they've met any. They play a large role in the demonology of the subject, beside self-righteous administrators and exploitative colonials. The only intellectually respectable response to a tin rattled in one's face by someone collecting for missionary work is a reasoned refutation of the whole concept of missionary interference. The documentation is there. Anthropologists point out, in their introductory courses to students, the excesses and short-sightedness of Melanesian missions that culminated in cargo-cults and famines. The Brazilian orders in the Amazon are charged with trading in slaves and child prostitutes, stealing land and intimidating the natives with force and threats of Hellfire. Missions destroy traditional cultures and self-respect, reducing peoples all over the globe to the state of helpless, baffled morons living on charity and in economic and cultural thraldom to the West. The great dishonesty lies in exporting to the Third World systems of thought that the West itself has largely discarded.

All this was in the back of my mind when I reached the American mission at N'gaoundere. It was something of a betrayal of anthropological principles even to be talking to missionaries: anthropologists have been obsessed with keeping themselves free of this taint since Malinowski, self-styled inventor of fieldwork, first issued his impassioned cry to the ethnographer to get up off the mission veranda and go out into the villages. Still, I would be on my guard against the devil's wiles and might save myself much time by talking to people who had actually lived in Do-wayoland.

To my great surprise, I was received with much warmth. Far from being rampant cultural imperialists, I found the missionaries except for one or two of the old school – to be extremely diffident about imposing their own views. Anthropology seemed, in fact, to be accorded a rather embarrassingly high position as a sovereign remedy against unfortunate cultural misunderstandings – a position which I could not honestly have claimed for it.

My original contact was Ron Nelson, who ran a mission radio studio whose programmes were distributed over much of West Africa – when the transmitters were not being nationalized by any particular government. He and his wife radiated a sort of calm strength far removed from the god-squad hysteria I had rather expected; after all, anyone who went out to Christianize the heathen must be a religious fanatic. I certainly found the latter among some of the more extreme groups working in Cameroon, people who railed against me for taking a couple of fertility dolls back to Europe on the grounds that I was importing the devil into God's territory; they should be burnt, not exhibited. Fortunately they were in the minority and, it seemed, a declining one if the younger missionaries I met were anything to go by.

On the whole, it was surprising how much work was being done on the local cultures and languages, translation work, pure linguistic research and attempts to adapt liturgy to local symbolic idiom; my own research would have been quite impossible without the mission's support. My funds having now been incautiously committed to the maw of an African bank, it was thanks to a loan from the mission that I was able to set myself up for the field in the first place. When I was ill, the mission hospital patched me up. When I was stranded, the missionaries put me up. When I ran out of supplies, they let me buy at their store which was theoretically only for their own personnel. To the jaded, ravenous fieldworker this was an Aladdin's cave of imported goodies at reduced prices.

But the mission was not only an emergency support for an anthropologist totally unprepared both materially and mentally for the bush, it was an all-important sanctuary where, when things simply became too much, one could flee, eat meat, talk English and be with people for whom the simplest statement did not have to be prefixed by long explanations.

The French missionaries also took me somewhat under their wing, clearly taking the view that we Europeans must stand together in the face of Americans. My favourite was Père Henri, a jolly, energetic extrovert. He had lived for a number of years with the nomadic Fulani and, as one of his colleagues put it, 'never been able to bring himself to preach to them'. He was totally in love with the people and spent hours discussing subtle points of grammar with so-called 'pure Fulani' speakers. His room at the seminary out in the hills was a shrine and a laboratory. With the aid of the most amazing Heath Robinson devices he collected recordings from ethnographic informants, edited them, typed them up and cross-referenced them all with switches operated by a swipe of the elbow, a stamp of the foot, a bang of the knee. He was a man who seemed to rev at twice the speed of normal mortals. On hearing that I was after a vehicle for the bush, he immediately whisked me off on a whistlestop tour of his contacts that involved viewing a number of broken-down jalopies at inflated prices. We ended up at the airport bar, run by a typical French colonial who turned out to be a Cockney who knew a man who knew a man, etc. By the end of the afternoon cars were coming round for the second time and Père Henri had negotiated a complicated series of options and prerogatives with insurance I could fill in for myself to cover anything under the sun. In the end I bought Ron Nelson's car with money loaned from the mission and piled in some mission supplies, fully intending to take off immediately for the field. Various people had lent me material they had accumulated from the mission's twenty-odd years in Dowayoland, not just linguistic information but outlines of kinship organization (wildly wrong) and all manner of ethnographic odds and ends that enabled me to convince the Dowayos that I knew far more about their culture than I was letting on and would detect half-truths and evasions as easy as winking. I had corresponded with two Summer Institute of Linguistics researchers while still in England who had furnished me with a word-list, an outline of the verb system and the basic phonemes, so I felt as well equipped as anyone needed to be. I fondly pictured myself heading out into the bush the next morning, the air clean and fresh, to begin from scratch a ruthlessly profound analysis of the culture of my very own primitive people. It was at this point that bureaucracy laid me low again.

The existence of a huge, antiquated French administrative system in an African cultural climate is a combination fit to defeat the most assiduous. It was broken to me gently by my hosts, with a form of bemused tolerance reserved for the innocent or dull-witted, that I could not leave town in my Peugeot 404 without sorting out the papers. At various points there would be gendarmes with nothing on their minds but the inspection of documents. Since it was impossible to tell in advance which could read and which could not, attempting to bluff one's way past was something to be undertaken only in an emergency.

I trooped off to the *préfecture* with the required documents in my hand. Then began the most convoluted and bizarre paper-chase. I was told I would be charged £120 registration fee, and after only a small amount of the by now expected jostling and arrogance I secured a piece of paper to take to the Finance Ministry who rejected it on the grounds that it did not have 200 francs' worth of fiscal stamps on it to pay administration costs. Fiscal stamps, under rules apparently spontaneously invented for that day alone, could only be purchased at the post office at the counter marked 'parcels'. The post office had no fiscal stamps for any sum less than 250 francs, so I attached one of these. At the Finance Ministry this was held to be improper and contrary to good administrative order. The Inspector would have to decide what to do. Alas, it was to be regretted that the Inspector was 'detained at lunch on business' but he would surely return. He did not return that day. I found a fatalistic Fulani taxi driver, similarly becalmed, who drew great comfort from his Muslim religion in this time of adversity. He was also involved in a major campaign to pay his electricity bill and rushed from one office to another trying to catch both off their guard. He was greeted with growing disapproval and I guessed that it was as punishment for his indecent haste that my piece of paper was finally stamped by competent authorities and I moved on to the next stage, after a mere three hours. Returning the next day, I revisited the office I had started from and exchanged all my pieces of paper for yet another in triplicate; these I exchanged after some hours for several more that I had stamped over on the other side of town (with but a short detour to buy more fiscal stamps). At the

31

Finance Ministry the taxi driver was still there, deep in prayer, convinced that only direct supernatural intervention could aid him. I sped on past.

By the end of the following day I had spent something like £200 and was approaching the end of my Odyssey. The man who had sent me off initially received me with great amusement at the *préfecture* and shooed other clients out of his office to offer me a chair. 'Congratulations,' he said with a huge grin. 'Most people take much longer than that. Have you the documents, the receipts and the declaration?' All these were swiftly produced. He slipped them into a folder. 'Thank you. Drop by next week.' Rather melodramatically, I recoiled in horror. He smiled beatifically. 'We have run out of registration cards, but expect them within a few days.' It is some indication that I had begun to adapt that I stood my ground, argued with force and venom and left the office with a temporary card and the entire folder in my possession.

The drive to Gouna, my turn-off, was through torrential rain and quite uneventful. The road was tarmac and, by local standards, good. Having been warned of certain of its more interesting features, I drove slowly as I descended from the plateau on to the plain and the temperature rose as if I were driving into an oven. One of the principal hazards of driving in the area is road-safety features. For example, there are a number of bridges which are only wide enough for one-way traffic. To ensure that drivers do not approach these at incautious speed, the authorities have judiciously placed a double line of bricks across the road – in those days without warning signs – on either side of the bridge. The burnt-out wrecks of cars and trucks whose drivers were unaware of this precaution are littered about the river beds. Many of them were killed. Spotting the new wrecks on the road was a standard way of relieving the boredom of driving through the featureless scrub. When one travelled by bush-taxi, each wreck was the occasion for a new story from the inevitable well-informed fellow passenger. Over there was a truck from Chad that had burst into flames because the petrol tank had been split open. That was the carcass of the motorbike ridden by two Frenchmen. They had been travelling at over eighty miles an hour when they hit the bricks and one had been impaled on the railings of the bridge.

Lest the seasoned traveller become too blasé, the authorities would also mark out areas of soft tarmac with granite boulders that were invisible at dusk. At a later stage one of these nearly cost myself and some friends our lives.

But for the moment I drove the two hundred kilometres quite contentedly, this being my first close look at the bush with its villages of mud huts, waving children and heaps of yams for sale by the roadside. It was now high wet season in late July and the landscape was a mass of stunted green bushes and grass. The bushfires of the dry season ensured that no real trees ever properly established themselves, and in the distance I could see the mountains of the Godet range, jagged teeth of bare granite, where the Dowayos lived.

Some hours later I reached Gouna and searched in vain for the petrol-station marked on my map. It simply did not exist. There is a great difference between any landscape as represented on a British map of the ordnance survey type and the French map with which I had equipped myself. Unlike its British counterpart, it told me little about river-crossings and whether churches had steeples or spires but dwelt expansively on restaurants and noble prospects. From my French map, it would have seemed that I was destined to move easily from one place of sensual delight to another.

For the first ten miles or so the dirt road was comparatively easy going. To either side of me stretched well-tended fields of what I clearly identified as maize and turned out to be millet, interspersed with areas of blackened scrubland. There, at last, hoeing contentedly in their gardens to either side of the road, were the people I had come to see, the Dowayos. First impressions were favourable. They smiled and waved, pausing in their endeavours to follow my passage up the road with their eyes and fell to lively discussion – clearly attempting to identify me. The road gradually became worse and worse until it was just a series of shattered boulders and deep craters. I had clearly wandered from the track. At this point two small boys hurried up carrying their shoes on their heads to protect them from the mud. To my relief they spoke French. This was indeed the road. Was it not very bad? It had been better. I learnt later that the funds for its repair had mysteriously disappeared. The *sous-préfet* had, about the same time, bought a large, low, American car. It was held to be poetic justice that the state of the road prevented him driving it to town. I gladly gave the boys a lift to their school, which they assured me was just up the road. As we bucked and juddered along, we took on various others until I had a fine collection of seven or eight.

Having finally met my Dowayos, I was at something of a loss for conversation. 'You are all Dowayos?' I inquired. There was a stunned silence. I repeated the question. As one, they roared with outrage. Haughtily, they disclaimed any kinship with that debased race of sons of dogs. They, it seemed, were Dupa. It was implied that no one but an idiot could confuse the two. The Dowayos lived over the other side of the mountain. Our conversation was over. Some ten miles or so further on they disembarked at their school, still looking somewhat affronted, and thanked me politely. I soldiered on alone.

According to my map, Poli should be a town of some size. True, there was no indication of population, but it was a *sous-préfecture*, had a hospital, two missions, a petrol-station and an airstrip. Even on large-scale English maps it had featured prominently. In my mind's eye it assumed the proportions of a town like Cheltenham, but with somewhat less imposing architecture.

It was quite simply a small village. The single street stretched for a couple of hundred yards with mud and aluminium sheet shacks on either side. Finally, it just ran out of steam in a tangle of undergrowth and a flagpole. I turned round, looking for the rest of it; there wasn't any. It had the air of a Wild West town down Mexico way during the siesta. A few ragged figures sidled about the streets and stared at me. A tin sign announced the presence of a bar, a depressing shanty tricked out in advertisements for the national lottery and the campaign against illiteracy. It was full of snappy expressions such as: 'The illiterate adult, incapable and lacking information, has always constituted an obstacle to the setting of any initiative tending towards the general upliftment of a country.' It was not clear how illiterates were supposed to read the placard. The bar was deserted but I slumped down on a stool and waited, glumly considering the sea of mud that made up the street.

Bars the world over are the place to go to get the feel of a town and the general lie of the land; this was no exception. After about ten minutes a furtive-looking man appeared and told me there was no point in my sitting there as they had run out of beer three weeks ago but the truck was expected within twenty-four hours. I was by now familiar with the disease of optimism and left, with directions to the Protestant mission.

This turned out to be a collection of tin-roofed houses such as I had come to recognize as the general mission style, grouped round a church of breeze blocks with a corrugated spire. The establishment was run by a wild-eyed American pastor and his family who had been in the business for some twenty-five years. It was an offshoot of the N'gaoundere mission and they had kindly offered to put me up until I got settled in a village. One thing had puzzled me: whenever I asked about the Poli mission people were immediately shifty or evasive. They spoke of the strains of the bush, the isolation, the heat. The first time I saw Pastor Brown, things began to fall into place. (Pastor Brown is not his real name and you can regard him as a fictitious character if you like.)

A bizarre figure sailed forth from the house, naked to the waist and exhibiting a huge paunch. On his head was a solar topee of imperial stamp, the effect of which was rather at variance with the bright purple sunglasses beneath. In his hand he bore a huge bunch of keys and a spanner. In the entire time I knew Herbert Brown I don't think I ever heard him finish a sentence, even though he used three languages simultaneously, switching from English to Fulani to French and back in the space of four words. A short, rapid burst of speech would be cut off by a Fulani oath, a gesture, a complete change of subject. His life-style was similar. He would punctuate a Bible class with welding a bicycle frame in the garage that was all his joy, abandoning this to rain blows on the aged generator of the station that was acting up, rushing off to dispense cough medicine at the house before the effectiveness of beating the generator had been established, and being waylaid before he got there by the need to chase goats from his garden or deliver a homily on the evils of debt. All this was accompanied by great screams and cries of rage, despair and frustration that turned him crimson in the face and led one to fear for his life. He believed fervently in the Devil with whom he was locked in a bitter personal combat. This explained why everything he tried to do for the people came to nought. The tractors he imported fell to pieces, the pumps broke down, the buildings fell apart. His life was an unabating whirlwind of struggle against entropy – making do, mending, borrowing a bit from here to bodge that, using this to hold that down, sawing, cutting, hammering, beating.

The station was engulfed in an atmosphere of manic tension that was totally opposed to that of the nearby Catholic mission; there, all was calm and well ordered. A single French priest ran the mission with his two 'mothers', nuns who dispensed medicine. There were even flowers. The Dowayos explained this by pointing out that the Protestant was a blacksmith. Among the Dowayos, blacksmiths are a separate group, contacts with whom have to be strictly regulated. They cannot marry other Dowayos, nor eat with them, draw water with them or go into their houses. They are disruptive because of their noise and smell and the strange way they speak.

5   Take me to your Leader

Days begin early in Africa. In my London life I had been used to
rising about half past eight of a morning; here everyone was
afoot at five-thirty, as soon as it was light. I was wakened
punctually by sounds of beating metal and screaming and guessed
that my local missionary was about his business. I had been
allocated a large, old mission house to myself. At the time I had
no idea what luxury I was enjoying; this was the last time I was to
see running water, not to mention electricity. I was intrigued to
find a paraffin refrigerator next door, the first time I had seen
one of these monsters. Capriciously unpredictable, these erstwhile
staples of bush life have become rare and expensive as electricity
has been introduced into the towns. Out of sheer perversity, they
will spontaneously defrost and destroy a month's meat supply or
give out so much heat as to incinerate anyone in the room. They
must be protected from draughts, damp, unevenness of the floor
and with luck they may consent to exert a mild cooling effect. In
Cameroon, with numerous languages and pijins, there are other
dangers. English paraffin and petrol get mixed up with French
pétrole and *essence*, American kerosene and gas. It is not unknown for helpful servants to top paraffin refrigerators up with
petrol, with devastating results. I peered inside; carefully stacked
were bags of large yellow termites. Even in death they seemed to
seethe. I was never able to bring myself to eat more than one or
two of these African delicacies, of which Dowayos are inordinately fond. The insects swarm at the beginning of the rains and
are attracted by any light. The standard means of collecting them
is to place a light in the midst of a bucket of water. When they
reach the light, the insects drop their wings and fall into the water
whence they can be collected and their fatty bodies either roasted
or eaten raw.

After a day's respite it was time to deal with the administration again. At the N'gaoundere mission I had been urged not to forget to register with the local police and to introduce myself to the local *sous-préfet*, the government representative. Accordingly, I armed myself with all my documents and set off on foot into town. Although it was something less than a mile, it was clearly a major eccentricity for a white man to walk. One man asked me whether my car had broken down. Villagers rushed out and shook hands with me jabbering in garbled Fulani. I had learned the rudiments of this tongue in London so I was able at least to say, 'I am sorry, I do not speak Fulani.' Since I had practised this sentence many times, it came out rather fluently and added to the incomprehension.

The police post was manned by about fifteen gendarmes, all armed to the teeth. One was polishing a sub-machine gun. The commandant turned out to be a huge Southerner of about six foot five. He summoned me into his office and inspected my documents minutely. What was my reason for being here? I displayed my research permit, a most impressive document, covered with photographs and stamps. He was clearly very unhappy as I tried to expound the essential nature of the anthropological endeavour. 'But what's it for?' he asked. Choosing between giving an impromptu version of the 'Introduction to Anthropology' lecture course and something less full, I replied somewhat lamely, 'It's my job.' Subsequently, I came to realize what a highly satisfactory explanation this was to an official who spent most of his life in pointlessly enforcing rules that seemed an end in themselves. He considered me lengthily under hooded eyes. I noticed for the first time that he was chewing on a needle. He would balance it, blunt end outwards, on his tongue. With a deft flick, he drew it wholly inside his mouth and performed an adroit adjustment so that it reappeared at the other side of the mouth with the point outwards. Back in, and there was a blunt end again. It was horribly like a snake's tongue. I felt there would be problems here, and I was to be proved right. For the time being, however, he let me go with the air of one allowing a rogue enough rope to hang himself. My name and personal details were recorded in a large volume that recalled the tomes of prohibited persons from the Embassy.

The *sous-préfet* lived in a dank and peeling house dating from the French colonial period. Moss and mould clung to every crack and crevice in its façade. On a hill above the town he had constructed a gleaming new palace but it stood empty, its air-conditioning unused, its tiled floors untrodden. Several explanations were given for this. Some said that the government had confiscated it as proof of corruption. The Dowayos, when I got to know them, told a different tale. The house had been built on an old Dowayo burial ground, despite their protests. They had not threatened, they claimed, they did not need to; they knew the spirits of their ancestors. They had simply informed the *sous-préfet* that the day he moved in was the day he would die. Either way, he never did move in but was doomed to look at his new house from the window of the old.

Having listened to my tale, a dour servant showed me in. I was struck by the fact that he knelt down before daring to address his superior.

I had been tipped off in advance that a present of some cigars would be 'acceptable', so these were duly produced and graciously accepted, disappearing swiftly inside the flowing robes. I was still standing up, the servant was still on his knees, the *sous-préfet* sat. My documents were once more examined with minute attention. I began to fear that they might wear out before I left the country. 'Out of the question,' he declared impassively. 'I cannot have you in Poli.' This was something of a setback; I had regarded this as a courtesy visit. 'But my research permit, from Yaounde,' I emphasized carefully, 'gives me permission to be here.' He lit one of my cigars. 'Yaounde is not here. You have not my permission.' Clearly this was not a situation where the passage of currency between us would be politic since the venerable retainer was still on his knees, taking in every word. 'How might I obtain your permission?' I persisted. 'A letter from the prefect, absolving me of responsibility, would be sufficient. He is to be found in Garoua.' He turned away and busied himself with papers. Our interview was at an end.

Back at the mission, Pastor Brown seemed to regard this as a vindication of his pessimism. He was touchingly cheered by my misfortune. He doubted whether I would ever get to see the prefect even if he happened to be where they claimed he was and not away in the capital; it was virtually certain he would not return for months. His own life had been fraught with many such frustrations. There was no hope; this was Africa. He walked off chuckling.

Calculating that I had just enough petrol to reach Garoua, about a hundred miles away, I resolved to set off at dawn the following day.

When I left the house next day, I was rather taken aback to find a sea of expectant faces confidently intending to accompany me. It has always been something of a mystery how such information circulates. Westerners often fail to realize with what minute attention they are observed. Being seen checking the fuel level is enough to trigger a barrage of requests for transport. To refuse is held to be inadmissible. Those who reproach Europeans with paternalism fail totally to perceive the relations that traditionally exist between rich and poor in much of Africa. A man who works for you is not just an employee: you are his patron. It is an open-ended relationship. If his wife is ill, that is as much your problem as his and you will be expected to do all in your power to heal her. If you decide to throw anything away, he must be given first refusal on it. To give it to someone else would be most improper. It is almost impossible to draw a line between what is your concern and what is his private life. The unwary European will get caught up in the vast range of loose kinship obligations, unless he is very lucky indeed. When an employee calls you 'father', this is a danger sign. There is surely a story about an unpaid dowry or dead cattle to follow and it will be perceived as a genuine betrayal not to assume part of the burden. The line between 'mine' and 'thine' is subject to continual renegotiation and Dowayos are as expert as anyone else in trying to get as much as they can out of a link with a rich man. The failure to realize that the relationship is being seen in very different terms from either side has led to much friction. Westerners are always complaining of their workers' (they are not called

'boys' or 'servants' nowadays) 'cheek' or 'nerve' in their bland
expectation that employers will look after them and always bail
them out when in trouble. Initially, I was much put out on occasions such as that which now presented itself. It seemed as if I
could never do anything spontaneously or go anywhere without
dragging a huge burden of obligation behind me. When in the
city, it was even more galling to find that people one had given
lifts to would be most annoyed if loans to finance their stay were
not also readily forthcoming. I had brought them to this strange
place; to forsake them here would be unthinkable.

However, on the first occasion I understood none of this and
embarked as many as seemed possible. Here again, European and
African notions are strongly divergent. By local standards, a car
with only six people in it is empty. Any claim that there is no
more room in it is greeted as a patent falsehood. It is a further
annoyance, having finally limited numbers by striking those
rather firm attitudes that Africans expect from Westerners who
really mean what they are saying, only to find that all manner of
baggage is suddenly dragged forth from concealment to be tied
to the roof with the inevitable strips of rubber cut from inner
tubes.

By now much delayed, I finally set off, the car heaving and
groaning, for Garoua. Various other features dependent on
numerous passengers soon became apparent. Dowayos are not
enthusiastic travellers and react badly to motion. Within ten
minutes, three or four of them were vomiting with great gusto all
over the car, none of them bothering to use the window for this
purpose. It was a decidedly seedy driver who finally reached the
city limits for more inspection of documents. Whereas a lone
white man attracts very little police attention, he is a matter of
some concern when hauling around Africans. The police were
very interested indeed in my movements and motives.

The appearance of the word 'doctor' on my passport seemed
to do more than anything else to dispel doubts, but my passengers
were not so lucky. While I was seeking to explain the absence of a
registration card for the car by leading the sergeant through the
dossier I had prudently brought from N'gaoundere, my passengers were dolefully lined up and required to produce receipts for

tax for the last three years, identity cards and membership cards of the sole political party. Inevitably, they fell somewhat short of perfection and this caused further delays. It became clear that little would be achieved before the midday siesta.

Garoua is a strange town situated on the River Benoue, a watercourse of sporadic appearance that varies from raging Mississippi in the rainy season to damp sand in the dry. Its dedication to its wayward river explains the smell of ripe fish that hangs over it like a pall of smoke. Dried fish is one of its main industries, the others being beer and administration. The beer is a particular source of fascination to Dowayos. They are keen customers of the breweries that produce the '33' beer, a mark of a previous French administration. Its peculiar quality is that it enables one to pass directly from sobriety to hangover without an intervening stage of drunkenness. The factory has a glass wall through which it was possible to see bottles of beer gliding, without the intervention of human agency, from one stage of the process to another. This deeply impressed the Dowayos and they spent hours watching the miracle. To describe it, they used the word *gerse* which means 'miracle', 'wonder', 'magic'. It was in this context that I first heard the term that was later so to occupy me as an anthropologist. It was also a fertile source of metaphor for their most metaphysical concepts. The Dowayos believed in reincarnation. It was like the beer at Garoua, they explained; people were like bottles that had to be filled with spirit. When they died and were buried, it was like sending the empty bottle back to the factory.

Fearing the worst, I now expected my encounter with the prefect, if it occurred at all, to take some days. A sort of calm fatalism had settled upon me. Things would take as long as they took; there was no point in worrying about it. It is one of the marks of the fieldworker that he has a supplementary gear into which he can shift at such moments and let the slings and arrows do their worst.

Not yet having made those contacts that stand the city-visiting anthropologist in such good stead, I checked into a hotel. Garoua boasted two of these, a modern Novotel at a mere £30 a night for the tourist trade and a seedy French colonial establishment for a fraction of that amount. The latter was clearly more my style. It had apparently been built for the rest and recreation of sun-crazed French officers from the forlorn stations of empire, and consisted of separate huts with grass roofs and furnished in military fashion; but it had water and electricity. It also possessed a large terrace on which the élite would sit and drink as the sun went down behind the trees. It was especially romantic since it was impossible to forget the presence of the rest of Africa: the roars of the lion in the zoo next door recalled it.

It was in this establishment that I first made the acquaintance of the woman who came to be known as the 'Coo-ee lady'. Whatever the season, Garoua is at least ten degrees hotter than Poli and, thanks to the river, has a profusion of mosquitoes. After being cloistered with vomiting Dowayos, I was therefore keen to have a shower. I was hardly under the tap when there came a persistent dry scratching noise at the door that ignored all attempts at interrogation. Swathing a towel round myself, I opened the door. Outside was an extremely large Fulani woman in her mid-fifties. She began simpering coyly, making little circular motions in the dust with her expansive feet. 'Yes?' I queried. She made drinking motions: 'Water, water.' My suspicions were aroused; dim memories of the rules of hospitality of the desert stirred. While I was considering the problem, she sailed blandly past me and seized a glass, filling it from the tap. To my horror she began to unwrap her vast form. The porter chose this moment to bring me some soap and, misinterpreting the situation, began to back out muttering apologies. I was trapped in a farce.

Fortunately, my few lessons in Fulani at the School of Oriental and African Studies stood me in good stead, and crying 'I do not wish it', I disclaimed any desire of physical contact with this woman, who reminded me strangely of Oliver Hardy. As if by some prearranged sign, the giggling porter seized one arm, and I the other and we got her outside. Thereafter she came back every hour, unable to accept that her charms were unappreciated and roamed outside calling 'Coo-ee', like a cat miaowing to come in. In the end, I tired of this. It was clear that she was operating in connivance with the management, so I declared that I was a missionary, come from the bush to see my bishop, and strongly disapproved of such goings-on. They were shocked and embarrassed; thereafter she ignored me.

The story became a favourite of the Dowayos as we sat around the fires in the evening when one of the chief occupations is spinning yarns. I had my assistant rehearse me in telling the 'fat Fulani woman story', as it came to be known, and when I got to the part where she called 'Coo-ee' they would scream with laughter, hug their knees and roll about on the ground. It did much to establish good relations between us.

My visit to the prefect's office the next day turned out to be an anticlimax. I was shown straight in. The prefect was a tall, very dark Fulani who listened to my problem, dictated a letter over the telephone and chatted to me most amiably about government policy with regard to establishing schools in pagan areas. The letter was brought to him, he signed it, stamped it and wished me good luck and 'bon courage'. Thus armed, I returned to Poli.

The first priority was to find an assistant and settle down to learning the language. The anthropologist's assistant is a figure who seems suspiciously absent from ethnographic accounts. The conventional myth seeks to depict the battle-scarred anthropologist as a lone figure wandering into a village, settling in and 'picking up the language' in a couple of months; at the most, we may find references to translators being dispensed with after a few weeks. Never mind that this is contrary to all known linguistic experience. In Europe, a man may have studied French at school for six years and with the help of language-learning devices, visits to France and exposure to the literature and yet find himself hardly able to stammer out a few words of French in an emergency. Once in the field, he transforms himself into a linguistic wonder-worker. He becomes fluent in a language much more difficult for a Westerner than French, without qualified teachers, without bilingual texts, and often without grammars and dictionaries. At least, this is the impression he manages to convey. Of course much may be done in pijin or even in English, but as often as not this isn't mentioned either.

It was clear to me that I needed a native Dowayo who also spoke some French. This meant that he would have been to school which also, given the nature of things in Dowayoland.

would imply that he was a Christian. For me that would be a considerable disadvantage since the traditional religion was one of the areas that interested me most. But there was nothing for it; I decided to go along to the local secondary school and see if they had someone suitably qualified. In fact, I never got there.

I was pre-empted by one of the preachers being trained at the Poli mission who knew what I was looking for; it so happened that he had twelve brothers. With rare entrepreneurial flair he swiftly mobilized them, marched them in from the village twenty miles out in the bush and presented them to me. This one, he explained was a good cook and very cheerful. Alas, he did not speak French. This one could read and write, was a terrible cook, but very strong. This one was a good Christian and told stories well. Each, it seemed, had great virtues and was an outstanding bargain. In the end, I agreed to hire one on trial, nobly settling for one who could not cook but spoke the best French, and could read and write. I realized at the time that the preacher himself was the man I should have taken on but his present employment prevented that. He was subsequently thrown out of the mission because of his promiscuous tendencies.

The time had come, if indeed it was not overdue, to move into a village. Dowayos divide into two sorts, mountain and plains. Everyone I had spoken to had urged me to live among plains Dowayos. They were less barbarous, supplies would be easier, more of them spoke French; I would be able to go to church more easily. Mountain Dowayos were savage and difficult, they would tell me nothing, they worshipped the Devil. Given such information, an anthropologist can only make one choice; I opted for mountain Dowayos. Some nine miles outside Poli was the village of Kongle. Although on the plains between two sets of hills, it was a mountain Dowayo village. Here, I was told, lived a very old man who was a stern traditionalist and had much arcane knowledge from the ancestors. The road was just passable. I decided to install myself here.

I consulted Matthieu, my new assistant. He was horrified to hear that I intended to live in the bush. Did this mean I should not have a fine house and other servants? Alas, it did. But surely I did not intend to live in Kongle – the people were savages. I should leave it to him; he would speak to his father, a plains Dowayo, who would arrange for us to live near the Catholic mission. I explained again the nature of my work. The only similar endeavour in Dowayoland had been the establishment of the linguists who had begun the analysis of the Dowayo language. They had spent some two years building a fine cement house and had been supplied by aeroplane. Matthieu was distressed to learn that my operation was much more a shoestring affair. It became clear that his status was dependent on my own, and he managed to make any lapse from dignity on my part seem like a bitter betrayal.

The moment for initial contact had come. Taking Matthieu's advice I brought some beer and tobacco and we set off for Kongle. The road was not too bad, though there were two rivers I did not much like the look of; indeed they proved rather a nuisance. My car would make a habit of developing faults half-way across. This was more serious than it might otherwise have been since they were liable to flash-flood. The mountains were pure granite, and should it rain there the water came straight off and caused almost a tidal wave in the river valleys. To either side of the road were fields with people working in them. They stopped and stared as we crawled past. Some fled. Later I found that they had assumed we were from the *sous-préfet*; outsiders usually meant trouble to Dowayos. At the foot of the mountains the road simply came to an end, and behind a palisade of millet stalks and cacti lay the village.

Dowayo huts are circular mud constructions with conical roofs. Being built of the mud and grass of the countryside, they assume a picturesque quality that is a relief after the ugliness of the cities. On the roofs grow long, trailing melons like the rambling roses of an English cottage. Following Matthieu's lead, I entered the circle that stands before every Dowayo village. This is the place where all public meetings and courts of law are conducted, where rituals are held and the various shrines important in religious life are to be found. Behind it lies a second circle where the communally owned cattle are kept. We passed through these and into the courtyard of the chief. It is not strictly accurate to use this term: the Dowayos have no real chiefs in the sense of leaders with power and authority. The French tried to create such men so that they would have figureheads to rule through and someone to collect taxes. The Dowayo term for such men, *waari*, is based upon an older classification. Chiefs are simply rich men, that is, men with cattle. Such men can organize the various religious festivals that are an essential part of ritual life. Poor men can associate themselves with rich celebrants and so complete rituals that they would not otherwise be able to afford. Chiefs are therefore very important people. Some have modelled themselves on the dominant local tribe, the Fulani, and sought to improve their status by refusing to speak Dowayo to their own people. They pretend that they can only understand it with difficulty, although it is their first language. Hence their astonishment when I refused to talk Fulani, like all the other white men, and insisted on learning Dowayo. Several of the chiefs have adopted all the panoply of pomp with which Fulani nobles surround themselves. They wear swords and have someone carrying a red sunshade over their heads. Some even have praise singers who precede them beating drums and wailing out a stereotyped list of their singular accomplishments and virtues, always in Fulani.

The Chief of Kongle was a rather different kettle of fish. He despised such acculturated Dowayos and made a point of only speaking Dowayo to them.

We came to a halt before a bare-breasted woman who knelt down before me and crossed her hands in front of her genitals concealed by a minute bunch of leaves. 'She is greeting you,' whispered Matthieu, 'shake hands with her.' I did so and she began to rock backwards and forwards on her heels crooning 'Thank you' repeatedly in Fulani and clapping her hands together. Faces appeared furtively over walls and round the side of huts. To my huge embarrassment a child appeared with a single folding chair and stood in the middle of the courtyard. I was required to sit. There was nothing else for it; I sat in splendid isolation, feeling rather like one of those stiff and very British figures in the photographs from colonial days. Status differences are clearly marked in much of Africa; Africans go in for heavy overstatement. People grovel and scrape, kneel and bow in a way that Westerners find hard to swallow; yet to refuse to accept such gestures is extremely impolite. Initially, whenever I would sit on a rock at the same level as everyone else it would cause acute embarrassment. People would desperately attempt to arrange matters so that they were lower than me or insist that I sit on a mat. Sitting on a mat, though lower than on a rock, carries higher status. Thus a compromise was reached.

By now the silence was becoming very strained and I felt it incumbent upon me to say something. I have already said that one of the joys of fieldwork is that it allows one to make use of all sorts of expressions that otherwise are never used. 'Take me to your leader,' I cried. This was duly translated and it was explained that the Chief was coming from his field.

Zuuldibo later became a good friend. He was in his early forties, invariably grinning all over his face, and somewhat running to fat. He was resplendent in Fulani robes, a sword and sunglasses. I now realize that whatever he had been up to when I arrived had not been in his field. No one cultivated the land in such attire; moreover, Zuuldibo had never touched a hoe in his life. He found the whole business of agriculture so unspeakably boring that he looked pained if anyone even mentioned work in the fields to him.

I launched into my prepared speech, saying how I had come many miles from the land of the white men because I had heard of the good ways of the Dowayos and especially of the good nature and kindness of the people of Kongle. This seemed to go down rather well. I wanted to live among them for a while and learn their ways and language. I made great play of the fact that I was not a missionary, which no one believed initially because I was living at the mission and driving a car that they recognized as belonging to the mission. I was not connected with the government, which no one believed because I had been seen hanging around the *sous-préfecture*. I was not a Frenchman, which no one even understood; to Dowayos all white men are the same. However, they listened politely, nodding their heads and muttering 'It is good', or 'true, true'. It was swiftly agreed that I would return in one week and the Chief would have a hut for myself and accommodation for my assistant. We drank a beer together and I gave them some tobacco. Everyone looked ecstatic.

As I left, an old woman fell on the ground and embraced my knees. 'What did she say?' I asked. Matthieu giggled, 'She said God had sent you to hear our voice.' It was a better start than I had dared to hope for.

In the following week I made another trip to the city to lay in supplies and buy tobacco. The black Nigerian tobacco that Dowayos so like sells in Dowayoland for four times the price in Garoua. I bought a large bag of it to pay informants with. My financial situation remained acute. I had arranged for my salary to be sent from England to my Cameroonian account. Since it came from England, it was sent to the old capital of British Cameroons, Victoria, thence to Yaounde, thence to N'gaoundere, thence to Garoua. In fact it never made it; the bank at Victoria simply deducted ten per cent 'expenses' and returned it to England, leaving me biting my nails and building up an ever larger debt at the Protestant mission. It was impossible to contact the bank at Victoria; they simply ignored letters, and the phones did not work.

It was during this final trip that I caught malaria for the first time. It manifested itself initially as a mild, light-headed sensation as I left the city. By the time I reached Poli, I had double vision and could barely see the road. A high fever was accompanied by shivering bouts and red-hot knives in the belly.

One of the sadder aspects of the disease is that it causes loss of control of the sphincters; when you stand up, you urinate on your feet. Even worse, there is an almost infinite list of remedies, some of which merely offer protection against the disease, others cure it once contracted. Unluckily, the pills I swallowed so hopefully were not curatives and so my condition worsened and the fevers rapidly reduced me to a whimpering wreck. Pastor Brown passed by to draw encouragement from my physical dissolution and lent me some curatives, warning me that 'Out here you can never be sure anything's gonna work.' Work, however, they did and I was rather shakily back on my feet in time to move into the village as planned – not, however, until I had spent several fever-racked nights tormented by the bats that came down into the house through holes in the ceiling. Much has been written on the excellence of bats' navigation equipment. It is all false.

Tropical bats spend their entire time flying into obstacles with a horrible thudding noise. They specialize in slamming into walls and falling, fluttering onto your face. As my own 'piece of equipment essential for the field', I would strongly recommend a tennis racket; it is devastatingly effective in clearing a room of bats. Pastor Brown had taken the time to tell me that bats carried rabies. They occupied a large place in my fevered fantasies.

It was not until I packed up to leave that I found the house had been broken into and half my food stolen.

6 Is the sky clear for you?

After all these trials and tribulations, I had finally arrived among 'my' people, I had my assistant, I had a pen and paper. Having been faced with so many impediments, it was with something of a shock that I realized I was now in a position to 'do anthropology'. The more I regarded this concept, the less clear it became. If asked to produce a picture of someone about this business, I would be far from sure what he would be doing. All I could offer would be a man who might be climbing a mountain (on his way to 'do anthropology') or writing up notes (having 'done anthropology'). Obviously a fairly wide definition was required rather like 'learning a foreign language abroad'. Any time actually spent talking to Dowayos would be considered legitimate, I decided.

There were a number of problems about this. Firstly, I could not speak a word of their language. Secondly, there were no Dowayos in the village that first morning; they were all scattered about the fields, hoeing between the millet shoots. I spent the entire day inventing things that had to be done to make my hut an efficient place to work in.

The Chief had kindly lent me a large hut in a side-compound of his own area of the village. My immediate neighbours were two of his wives and his younger brother. It was only later that I realized he was showing considerable trust in assigning me such a position that would normally only be given to in-laws of a favourite wife. The previous incumbent had left a large number of unidentifiable little bundles, spears and arrowheads thrust into the thatch. (I could not help thinking of Mary Kingsley discovering a human hand in her hut while among the Fang.) Once removed, my equipment was disposed among the roof beams. I set up a map of Poli I had acquired in the capital. This was a major wonder to Dowayos who never grasped its principles and would ask me to tell them where to find villages I had never visited. When I was able to, they would ask me to name the people who lived there and could never understand why I could accomplish the first but not the second.

As another sign of special favour, the chief had assigned me two folding chairs such as I had seen on my first visit to the village. These proved to be the only chairs in the village and whenever a person of status visited the chief they would be hauled back to his hut. So they oscillated between us like a dinner jacket I had shared with three other undergraduates while at university.

My furniture was completed by a bed of beaten earth, quite the most uncomfortable bed I have ever encountered anywhere. I had bought, at huge expense, a thin mattress stuffed with cotton which the chief much coveted. Beds were all his ambition. He confided to me that he wished to die in an iron bed he could leave to his son. 'The termites will not be able to eat it,' he chuckled gleefully. 'They will go crazy.'

For the first three weeks the rain poured down with relentless fury. The very air was saturated. Mould grew on any exposed surface and I feared greatly for the lenses of my camera. Time was spent trying to learn the basis of the language. Africans are normally bi- or tri-lingual to some degree but have no experience, for the most part, of learning a language in anything but social encounters. The idea of recording a verb in all its forms, tenses, moods, to see the overall system is totally alien. They learn their languages as children and can switch effortlessly from one to another.

The Dowayos never could appreciate the difficulties their language offered to a fieldworker from Europe. It is tonal, that is, the pitch in which a word is spoken totally affects its meaning. Many African languages have two tones; the Dowayos had four. There was no difficulty in telling a high tone from a low but in the middle, it seemed, anything could happen. The matter was complicated by the fact that Dowayos also combine tones to form glides and a tone may well be affected by the tones of neighbouring words. Added to this were dialect problems. Some areas collapse tones together as well as using different vocabulary and syntax. Since what counts is relative tone, I found it initially hard to switch from talking to a woman with a high-pitched voice to a man whose high tones might be about the same level as a woman's low tones. What really depressed me was a routine that became standard. I would meet a Dowayo and greet him. There was no problem about this; I had made my assistant school me long and hard in 'Is the sky clear for you?' 'The sky is clear for me, is it clear for you?' 'The sky is clear for me too', which had to be gone through for each person you were greeting. The English tend to set little store by these rituals, regarding them as an empty waste of time, but the Dowayos are not hurried like ourselves and easily take offence if they are neglected. I would then make some remark of a fairly inane kind such as 'How is your field?' or 'Have you come far?' Their faces would drop and they would look puzzled. My assistant would step in and say – to my own ear – exactly what I had just said. Their faces would light up. 'Aaagh. I understand' (pause). 'But how is it he does not speak our tongue? He has been among us for two weeks.'

The Dowayos have such a low view of their own tongue, their own chiefs refusing to use this crude, unsubtle instrument, little better than animal cries, that they cannot understand how anyone could fail to learn it. Consequently they make poor linguistic informants. The temptation to use the trade language, Fulani, was enormous. I had learnt a little of this in London where all manner of learning aids, dictionaries and manuals are available. There is a strong tradition, however, that information 'doesn't count' unless gleaned in the native tongue and it was certainly true that I had found all sorts of distortions in the data collected in Fulani, which carves up the area of unclean occupations 'blacksmith, undertaker, barber, circumciser, healer' in a very different way from Dowayo. According to all the information I had received, these were all undertaken by the same person whereas 'priests' were set apart. In fact, in Dowayo, it is the blacksmith who is the most separate and the other tasks are distributed according to quite different criteria. There is also the consideration that Dowayos do not normally talk Fulani among themselves. There was, admittedly, one man in my village who refused to talk anything else even to his friends, but this was a standard joke of the kind Dowayos get themselves bogged down in. He would complain loudly when labouring with other Dowayos in the fields. How was it that he, a noble Fulani, was obliged to labour with savage pagans? He would elaborately recount the manifold faults of this race of dogs amid growing hysteria until there came a point at which people would begin to fall about with laughter and gasp for breath. It was considered highly amusing that I always insisted on talking to him in my own poor Fulani, and sometimes we would conduct a sort of double-act.

Extended use of the trade language would have had numerous disadvantages. I could certainly have conducted interviews in it, but never real conversations. Dowayos speak a bastardized form of Fulani with all the irregular forms ironed out. The sense of the words is often changed by accommodation to Dowayo concepts. Moreover, it is only by being capable of following their own tongue that it is possible to grasp those asides that may be intended for other ears.

On one occasion, I trekked up into the mountains to the outermost confines of Dowayoland. Many of the children had never seen a white man before and began to scream with terror until comforted by their elders who explained that this was the white chief from Kongle. We all laughed good-naturedly at their fright and smoked together. Normally I do not smoke, but found it useful to be able to do so to share tobacco and so create a social bond between us. As I left, one of the girls burst into tears and I heard her snivel, 'I wanted to see him take his skin off.' I made a mental note to ask about it later; normally, such expressions turned out to be the result of a misinterpreted tone or an unknown homonym. When asked about it, however, my assistant showed acute embarrassment. I went into a jollying-along routine I had had to develop for precisely this sort of situation and gave him all my attention; Dowayos are frequently mocked by surrounding tribes for their 'savagery' and will clam up at the least sign that they are not being taken seriously. Reluctantly, he confessed that Dowayos believed that all white men who lived for extended periods in Dowayoland were reincarnated spirits of Dowayo sorcerers. Underneath the white skins we had managed to cover ourselves with, we were black. When I went to bed at night, I had been seen to take off my white skin and hang it up. When I went to the mission with the other white men, we drew the curtains at night, locked the door and took our white skins off. Of course, he declared somewhat sniffily, *he* did not believe this, looking me up and down as if afraid that I would revert to my black colour on the spot. The belief explained Westerners' obsession with privacy.

It also explained the annoyance sometimes manifested by Dowayos at my linguistic failings after months among them; they were regarded as pathetic attempts to disguise my essentially Dowayo nature. It was common knowledge that I was capable of understanding anything I really wanted to. Why did I insist on pretending the language was new to me? It was only after nearly a year in Dowayoland that I heard Dowayos refer to me as 'our' white man and felt a surge of pride. I felt sure that my attempts to master the language, incomplete and undervalued as they were, played a large role in my 'being accepted'.

But all this is with the benefit of hindsight. In those first three weeks all I knew was that I had undertaken to learn an impossible language, that there were no Dowayos in the village, that it was pouring with rain, and that I felt weak and terribly lonely.

Like most anthropologists in this situation, I sought refuge in collecting facts. The prevalence of factual data in anthropological monographs stems, I am sure, not from the inherent value or interest of the facts but from an attitude of 'when in doubt, collect facts'. This is, in a sense, an understandable approach. The fieldworker cannot know in advance what is going to prove important and what is not. Once one has recorded data in the notebook there is a strong disinclination to leave it out of the monograph; it is remembered in terms of miles walked in the sun, or hours spent trying to pin people down. Moreover, selection presupposes a coherent view of what one is trying to do and most anthropological monographs are written by someone whose aims are limited to 'writing an anthropological monograph' and no more.

So off I went every day, armed with my tobacco and notebooks and paced out the fields, calculated the yields, counted the goats in a flurry of irrelevant activity. This at least had the virtue of making my weird and inexplicable ways familiar to the Dowayos and I began to know them by name.

Much nonsense has been written, by people who should know better, about the anthropologist 'being accepted'. It is sometimes suggested that an alien people will somehow come to view the visitor of distinct race and culture as in every way similar to the locals. This is, alas, unlikely. The best one can probably hope for is to be viewed as a harmless idiot who brings certain advantages to this village. He is a source of money and creates employment. A turning-point in my own relations came after some three months, when the Chief intimated to me that he would like to regain possession of his hut. The matter was discussed at length and I agreed that the best solution was for me to have my own hut built. This cost me the princely sum of £14 and enabled me to employ the circumciser's son who vouched for my bona fides with his father, the chief's brother, who taught me about hunting, and the nephew of the local healer, who put me in touch with his uncle. My car served naturally as village ambulance and taxi. The women could always borrow salt or onions from me. The village dogs knew I was a soft touch and would congregate before my hut, much to the rage of my assistant. The potters and blacksmiths had never done so much business. My presence lent huge status to the Chief. He always made sure I knew about all the festivals so I could give him a lift to them. I acted as bank for those with no money but great expectations. I was expected to be a buying agency for those who needed parts for their bicycles or lamps. I was a source of medicine for the sick.

True, I had disadvantages. I attracted outsiders to the village, which was bad. I would fatigue my hosts with foolish questions and refuse to understand their answers. There was the danger that I would repeat things I had heard and seen. I was a constant source of social embarrassment. On one occasion, for example, I asked a man whether he had to refrain from sexual intercourse before going hunting. This was perfectly all right in itself, but his sister was within earshot Both he and she shot off in opposite directions emitting loud wailing noises. Seconds before, I had been sitting in the hut chatting to three men. In a flash, the hut was empty except for my assistant who was groaning and holding his head in his hands. The huge indecency I had committed was the subject of horrified whispers for weeks afterwards.

My rather wobbly control of the language was also a grave danger. Obscenity is never very far away in Dowayo. A shift of tone changes the interrogative particle, attached to a sentence to convert it into a question, into the lewdest word in the language, something like 'cunt'. I would, therefore, baffle and amuse Dowayos by greeting them, 'Is the sky clear for you, cunt?' But my problems were not exclusively with interrogative vaginas; similar problems haunted eating and copulation. One day I was summoned to the Chief's hut to be introduced to a rainmaker. This was a most valuable contact that I had nagged the Chief about for weeks. We chatted politely, very much sounding each other out. I was not supposed to know he was the rainmaker; I was the one being interviewed. I think he was much impressed by my respectful demeanour. We agreed that I would visit him. I was anxious to leave since I had acquired some meat for the first time in a month and left it in my assistant's care. I rose and shook hands politely, 'Excuse me,' I said, 'I am cooking some meat.' At least that was what I had intended to say; owing to tonal error I declared to an astonished audience, 'Excuse me. I am copulating with the blacksmith.'

The people in my village rapidly became versed in translating what I said into what I meant. How far my command of the language actually progressed and how far I managed to teach them my own particular pijin was difficult to say.

I remained convinced, however, that my chief value for the Dowayos was simply that of a curiosity. It is untrue that boredom is a complaint exclusively endemic to civilization. Village life in Africa is very dull indeed, not just to a Westerner accustomed to a wealth of daily-changing stimuli, but to villagers themselves. Every small event or scandal is lovingly rehashed and raked over, every novelty sought out, any change of routine greeted as a relief from monotony. I was liked because I had entertainment value. No one could ever be sure what I would do next. Perhaps I would go off to the city and bring back some new wonder or story. Perhaps someone would come and visit me. Perhaps I might go into Poli and find there was beer. Perhaps I would come up with some new foolishness. I was a constant source of conversation.

Having now invented all sorts of pointless activities in which to spend my time, I felt the need of a routine. It was essential to rise early. At this time of the year, most of the people slept in small shelters in the fields to guard against the ravages of cattle. In theory Dowayos are supposed to return their herds of cattle to the village corral at night, but they seldom bother. Traditionally, guarding and herding are done by small boys but nowadays these must be sent to school. The result is that cattle are allowed to wander about the fields and inflict great damage on the crops. A woman knows that if her field is ravaged this will be taken as proof of her adultery and her husband will beat her into the bargain; women are therefore especially vigilant guardians. With the risk to their food for the next year, few return to the village at all for weeks on end, and those that do are away very early.

I therefore tried to be afoot at first light to greet people before they left. 'Greeting people' is a great African tradition. It consists of being visited by people you do not know who then stay for hours and defeat all attempts at conversation. It is rude to make a hasty departure and so one goes over the same subjects again and again – the fields, the cattle, the weather. This has certain advantages for the neophyte: the vocabulary is small, the constructions simple and he is often able to surprise people with whole sentences he has learned off by heart.

Once 'greeting' had been accomplished to the satisfaction of all, I would start on breakfast. Food was a major problem in Dowayoland. I had a colleague who had worked in the southern jungle zone of Cameroon and told me great tales of the culinary delights that awaited me. Bananas would grow round my door, avocados fell from the trees as you walked along, meat was plentiful. Unfortunately, I was closer to the desert than the jungle. The Dowayos showered all their love upon millet. They could not eat anything else for fear of falling ill. They talked about millet; they paid debts in millet; they made beer from millet. Should one offer them rice or yams, they would eat them but regret bitterly that they were not as good as millet. With this, they ate a sour, glutinous vegetable sauce made from the leaves of wild plants. As an occasional diet this was all very well, but Dowayos ate it twice a day, morning and evening, every single day. Boiled millet is rather like polyfilla. They regretted that they could not sell me any.

Land is free in Dowayoland. A man may take as much as he likes and build his house wherever he chooses. This does not, however, lead to an agricultural surplus. A man cultivates as little as possible. Clearing the ground and harvesting are hard enough. Worst of all is the hoeing that is necessary half-way through the growing season. To relieve the tedium of this, great beer parties are given and the workers remain as long as there is beer to drink, then they wander off to another party taking their host with them. In this way, solitary work is punctuated by bouts of social drunkenness. Although millet fetches a good price in the cities, the Dowayos are not attracted to sell there. The market is controlled by Fulani traders who expect to make one or two hundred per cent profit on anything they touch. Since they also control transport, the remuneration a Dowayo cultivator would receive is very small indeed. Dowayos tend to grow enough for themselves and kinship obligations if there is a festival in the air. Otherwise margins are fairly tight and if the rains are less abundant than expected just before harvest, there may be famine. Trying to buy anything in Dowayoland is very much swimming against the current; the French deliberately introduced taxation, although unprofitable, to compel the Dowayos to use money. Even now, however, they prefer to barter and build up debts that can all be discharged in the slaughter of cattle than to deal in money. Had they given me millet, I should have had to pay back in meat or millet bought in the city.

Although they have cattle, the Dowayos do not milk them or breed them for food. They are dwarf cattle, without humps, unlike the Fulani cattle, and give almost no milk. Dowayos also claim that they are 'very fierce' although I saw no evidence of this Ideally they should be killed only for festivals. At the death of a rich man who has, say, forty cattle, ten or more should be killed and the meat given to kinsmen. Nowadays the central government tries to prevent what it regards as waste of resources, but the custom persists.

Other festivals involve killing cattle for the dead, and cattle must be paid to buy wives. Hence their wanton destruction for meat or money will be resisted by young men who have their eye on marriage prospects. Whenever I was given meat, especially by the Chief of Kongle, there was a rapid alternation between dearth and plenty. He would always insist on giving me a whole leg, which was far more than I could ever eat before it went rotten. So I would have a series of sub-letters of the Chief's hospitality to whom I could make over meat in return for eggs. Not that eggs were much of a blessing. Dowayos do not normally eat eggs; they regard the idea as mildly disgusting. 'Don't you know where they come from?' they would ask. Eggs are not something to be eaten but rather to be hatched into chickens. So it was that they would very kindly bring me eggs that they had kept for a couple of weeks in the hot sun, so I could indulge my sick fancy. Floating them like witches did not always suffice to screen out the bad ones; once eggs have got beyond a certain stage of putrescence they begin to sink in water like fresh ones. Many is the time that my hopes of eating eggs were dashed as I broke them, one by one, and smelt the thick stench rising from their bluish-green interiors.

Faced with the impossibility of eating off the land, I decided to keep my own chickens. This, also, was not a success. Some I bought, some were given to me. Dowayo chickens, on the whole, are scrawny, wretched things; eating them is rather like eating an Airfix model of a Tiger Moth. They responded to treatment, however. I fed them on rice and oatmeal, which Dowayos who never feed them at all found a huge extravagance. One day, they began to lay. I had fantasies of being able to eat an egg every day. As I sat in my hut, gloating over my first day's haul, my assistant appeared in the doorway, an expression of bland self-satisfaction on his face. '*Patron*,' he exclaimed, 'I just noticed the chickens were laying eggs so I killed them before they lost all their strength!'

After this, I tended to restrict myself to a breakfast of oatmeal and tinned milk which I bought in the mission shop. Tea is a major crop in Cameroon but it was normally impossible to buy it in Poli. There was, however, Nigerian tea, presumably smuggled over the border.

My assistant would normally eat with me since he claimed it was impossible to eat the food of these savage mountain Dowayos. After some months I noticed he had become hugely fat and discovered that he was in fact dining with both the Chief and myself.

After breakfast would come my 'clinic'. There is a great deal of disease in Dowayoland and I was something less than ecstatic about having it accumulate around my hut. However, even with my limited knowledge and medical resources, it would have been inhuman to turn the sick away as my assistant did initially. In accordance with African notions of status, he regarded me as someone who had to be carefully screened from contact with the common herd. It was all right for me to speak to chiefs or magicians but I should not waste my time with foolish commoners or women. He was frankly horrified when I talked to children. He posted himself strategically in front of my compound and would leap out on anyone who sought to approach me directly, interposing himself like a secretary in the ante-chamber of some great man. Whenever I sought to give anyone a cigarette, he would insist that it pass from my hand to his before it could be given to a Dowayo. In the end we had words about it and he desisted in his attentions but always managed to convey that excessive contact with ordinary people diminished his own exalted rank.

Infected wounds and sores would always be brought to me and I would put on anti-biotic and a dressing, knowing full well the futility of this since Dowayos always keep wounds open and remove a dressing as soon as they are out of sight. There were one or two cases of malaria, on which I now considered myself to be an expert, and I would hand out quinine, my assistant making sure I got the numerals right when I explained dosage.

The news soon got around that I was willing to hand out 'roots', as the Dowayos called remedies, for malaria and had good medicines. I was somewhat taken aback when an old woman turned up very angry and complained that I had given her malaria. A huge argument developed that I was quite unable to follow at this stage, and she was driven away with much mockery. It was only after months of work with healers and sorcerers that I understood what the trouble had been. Dowayos divide disease into a number of classes. There are 'epidemics', infectious diseases that white men have remedies against, things like malaria or leprosy. There is witchcraft of the head or from plants. There are the symptoms that are caused by the spirits of the dead. Lastly, there are pollution diseases that come from contact with forbidden things and people. The cure for the last is regulated contact with the forbidden thing or person that has caused the disease. Having heard that I had a cure for malaria, the old woman had imagined it was a pollution disease and the cure in my hut was also the cause of the disease. To keep such a powerful and dangerous thing in the middle of a village would, indeed, be grounds for complaint.

The rest of the morning would be spent on language learning. My assistant greatly enjoyed the role of teacher and took great delight in drilling me in verb forms until I could stand no more. He was rather less taken with a practice I adopted after the first couple of weeks.

I had with me a small, portable tape recorder that I nearly always carried with me; when talking to people in the fields I would sometimes record conversations. Dowayos loved to hear their own voices, but were not hugely impressed; they'd seen tape recorders before. Dowayo dandies affected radio-cassette players and most had encountered them at one time or another. What really had them murmuring 'wonder'. 'magic' was my writing. Except for a few of the children, Dowayos are illiterate. Even the children write in French and, before the linguists did research on the Dowayo tongue, it would never have occurred to anyone to write in Dowayo. When I made notes in a mish-mash of French and English with important Dowayo phrases copied in phonetic transcription, they would delightedly watch me for hours, taking turns to look over my shoulder. When after a couple of weeks I was able to read back to a man what he had said at our last meeting, he was stupefied. Gradually, I built up a library of taped conversations, my notes on them, and the interpretations I had received subsequently. I was able to pick one at random and go through it, word by word, with my assistant, making him justify translations he had given me, elaborate on certain terms or beliefs and explain the difference between close synonyms. Once this became a standard procedure, our level of linguistic competence rose enormously. He became much more careful; I began to learn much faster. Instead of just foisting me off with an approximation, he would mark down points of difficulty for us to go over later and abandoned the stance of omniscience he had adopted initially.

Lunch would be some form of hard-tack, perhaps chocolate, peanut butter, rice. Then my assistant would go off for a siesta during the hottest part of the day and I would retire to my rock-like bed for an hour's letter-writing, sleep or desperate calculation of my financial straits.

After some weeks the weather became much hotter, the rain came in sporadic downpours and I instituted the afternoon swim. Water is very dangerous in Dowayoland. A number of parasitic diseases are endemic, the worst being bilharzia. Many Dowayos suffer from it; it produces severe intestinal bleeding, leading to nausea, weakness and, finally, death. The life-expectancy in Dowayoland is so low anyway that many perish before it gets to this stage. I had been told many different things, at different times, by different people. According to some authorities, one foot injudiciously placed in a stream confers lifelong bilharzia; according to others, it is necessary to immerse oneself for hours in polluted water before infection is possible. A passing French geographer told me that the water was perfectly safe after the first heavy rains. These, it seemed, washed downstream the watersnails that carry the parasite. Thus, provided one avoided stagnant or slow-flowing water in the dry season, the risk was minimal. Since I had been tortured by the sight of Dowayos joyfully splashing in the cool streams while I laboured past bathed in sweat, I was greatly tempted to take the plunge; it was in any case impossible to travel far in Dowayoland without wading waist-deep across raging torrents. I therefore decided to accept the geographer's diagnosis and go to the men's bathing place, a deep pool in the granite rocks at the bottom of a waterfall, forbidden to women on the grounds that boys were circumcised here.

On the occasion of my first appearance at the swimming place, there were one or two young men on their way back from the fields who had stopped to wash. My anatomy was clearly the subject of florid speculation. On the following days there were twenty or thirty men who spontaneously appeared to see the great novelty of a white man with no clothes on. Thereafter, my value as an attraction tailed off rapidly and numbers returned to normal. I felt mildly insulted.

This place was delightful, set at the foot of the mountains from which the water gushed, cold and clean. The pool itself was shaded by trees and floored with sand. At various levels around the stream were ledges in the rock face on which one could lie in all possible variations of heat or cool.

Matthieu and I came here most days unless engaged elsewhere and it was in this all-male environment that the Dowayos first began to talk to me about their religion and beliefs. Since it was abundantly clear that they had all been circumcised after the Dowayo fashion and I had not, conversation turned spontaneously around this topic with which Dowayo culture has more than a passing obsession.

The bathing over, we would make a turn through the fields, trying to track down any beer parties being held that day. Here, beneath a woven shade, we would find anything up to twenty men and women intermittently hoeing and drinking. Millet beer has been described by an eminent French colonial official as having the consistency of pea soup and the taste of paraffin. The description is accurate. Dowayos take nothing else at midday and become remarkably drunk on its very low alcoholic content. This was a constant source of wonder to me. I had made an early policy decision to drink native beer despite the undoubted horrors of the process of fabrication. On my very first visit to a Dowayo beer party, this was put severely to the test. 'Will you have beer?' I was asked. 'Beer is furrowed,' I replied, having got the tones wrong. 'He said "Yes",' my assistant explained to them in a tired voice. They were amazed. No white man, at this time, had ever been known to touch beer. Seizing a calabash, they proceeded to wash it out in deference to my exotic sensibilities. This they did by offering it to a dog to lick out. Dowayo dogs are not beautiful at the best of times; this one was particularly loathsome, emaciated, open wounds on its ears where flies feasted, huge distended ticks hanging from its belly. It licked the calabash with relish. It was refilled and passed to me. Everyone regarded me, beaming expectantly. There was nothing to be done; I drained it and gasped out my enjoyment. Several more calabashes followed. They were astonished that I was not drunk. It is virtually impossible for a Westerner to get drunk on millet beer; he simply cannot hold the required amount. Dowayos, however, rapidly become falling-down drunk on factory-made beer. It is not uncommon for them to make a bottle last three days, during which time they claim to be constantly inebriated.

The Chief, Zuuldibo, was always hovering on these occasions; he never missed a beer-party, though he steadfastly refused to undertake agricultural labour in payment. The simplest way of finding one was to send out Matthieu to find Zuuldibo. Since Zuuldibo's dog had taken to following me in the hope of bounty, we made a rather bizarre procession. My first successful speech in Dowayo was: 'Matthieu follows the Chief. I follow Matthieu. The dog follows me.' This was held to be wit of the highest order and much repeated.

After a session in the fields, I would always try to be at the crossroads about nightfall as people returning to the various areas of Kongle passed by. A couple of felled trees had been brought here as seats and the men sat and gossiped and swatted mosquitoes until it was time to eat. A meal of oatmeal or instant mashed potato (very expensive but real potatoes rotted in days) with a can of soup finished off the day and I would retire to write up notes, record questions to ask the next day and read anything I could lay my hands on.

My one real luxury was a gas light I had bought in N'gaoundere. Although I had to drive 150 miles to change the cylinder, this only had to be faced every couple of months and I had a spare. It meant I could work after dark, a huge boon since night falls before seven o'clock all the year round. I was much visited by Dowayos wanting to see this wonder and had great difficulty explaining that it was *not* electricity.

So the first few weeks passed and I began to feel my way into village life. As the Dowayos began to drift back to the villages the edge was taken off my loneliness, but I was still subject to huge bouts of depression when trapped in my tiny hut by the rain. My health had not fully recovered from the attack of malaria. This was partly due to the monotony of my diet that often led me to skip meals or just to force as much down as I could by regarding food as essential fuel.

It was months before I felt I had made any progress in the language at all and I was quietly convinced that I would return having learned and understood nothing. The worst thing was that Dowayos seldom if ever seemed to *do* anything, have any beliefs or engage in symbolic activity. They just existed.

My frustration at not being able to follow more than a fraction of what was said around me began to focus on my hapless assistant. It seemed to me that he told me nothing but incorrect verb forms; I began to doubt whether half the time he understood what I was saying, even whether he was able to speak the dialect of mountain Dowayos at all. I had seen him, on occasion, exchange furtive looks with other men when certain topics were raised and I scented conspiracy.

The position of a fieldworker's assistant is a difficult one. He is expected by the locals to take their part in any clash of loyalties with his employer; in an African society the life of a man who incurs the wrath of his kinsmen can be made very uncomfortable indeed. At the same time, his employer expects him to act as his agent in dealing with local people and tipping him off on strategies and contacts. For an ethnographer, anxious for the truth, working through the medium of the convoluted loyalties of a partly literate schoolboy is a frustrating business; it is aggravated by the fact that each party may have quite different notions of what is expected of him. Most Dowayos, extrapolating from their experience of missionaries, expect white men to be fanatical Christians. They were very surprised, therefore, when my assistant went to prayer meetings on Sundays while I did not. I had to make a point of bumping into the Christians on their way back and spending time with them just to show that my absence was not from feelings of superiority on my part.

To begin with I was distressed to find that I couldn't extract more than ten words from Dowayos at a stretch. When I asked them to describe something to me, a ceremony, or an animal, they would produce one or two sentences and then stop. I would have to ask further questions to get more information. This was very unsatisfactory as I was directing their answers rather more than sound field method would have prescribed. One day, after about two months of fairly fruitless endeavour, the reason struck me. Quite simply, Dowayos have totally different rules about how to divide up the parts of a conversation. Whereas in the West we learn not to interrupt when somebody else is talking, this does not hold in much of Africa. One must talk to people physically present as if on the telephone, where frequent interjections and verbal response must be given if only to assure the other party that one is still there and paying attention. When listening to someone talking, a Dowayo stares gravely at the floor, rocks backwards and forwards and murmurs, 'Yes', 'It is so', 'Good', every five seconds or so. Failure to do so leads to the speaker rapidly drying up. As soon as I adopted this expedient, my interviews were quite transformed.

But the main problem lay not so much in my assistant's fidelity and honesty as in his age. Age brings status in Africa; the Dowayo way of showing respect is to address someone as 'old man'. Thus venerable Dowayo Nestors would call me 'old man' or 'grandfather'. It was scandalous that a mere child of seventeen should be present at the conversations of such learned elders as ourselves. He may have been fairly invisible to me, but to the Dowayos he stuck out like a sore thumb. In later days, he would be peremptorily dismissed by aged Dowayos before we got down to serious matters, and I would consult him later with any linguistic problems that had come up. Fortunately, he had some obscure kinship with the people of the principal rainchief and this sufficed to excuse his presence in the early days, otherwise I – like others who had worked among the Dowayos – would have returned huffily convinced of the pig-headed stubbornness of that race.

7 'O Cameroon, O Cradle of our Fathers'

The one break in the weekly routine was my Friday afternoon visit to town. Its justification was that I had to collect my mail which arrived from Garoua every Friday. This was a blatant falsehood: the mail only arrived *in theory* on Friday. The Fulani chief of Poli held the contract to deliver the post in his truck but when he did so, or whether he did so at all, depended entirely on personal whim. Should he decide that he wanted to spend a few days in the city, he would do so and the mail would not arrive for another week. It was a matter of supreme indifference to him that none of the schoolteachers or other functionaries received their pay, that drugs for the hospital would be held up, that the entire town would be inconvenienced.

Moreover, mail is so slow that the first two months all I received was letters from the bank in Garoua with outrageously inaccurate statements of my account. By some sleight of hand I now had three accounts, one in Yaounde, one in Garoua, and another, quite mysteriously, in a town I had never even visited.

An important feature of 'collecting the mail' was that it provided me with a break from my assistant. I had never in my life spent so much time in the uninterrupted company of one person and had begun to feel like one married against his will to a most unsuitable partner.

Hence Friday afternoons began with the cheerful filtering of water for my trip, which I insisted on undertaking on foot, firstly because petrol was impossible to obtain in Poli and so had to be carefully husbanded, secondly because otherwise I had to take the entire village. In the rainy season there was a copious flow of water so I contented myself with simply filtering it for drinking

68

purposes. In the dry season all waterholes become stinking stagnant pools and it is necessary to boil it or add chlorine. My water bottle became a great joke among the Dowayos who were amazed that I could make a litre last most of the day, but they accepted this as a peculiarity of the white man. In fact, they have their own system of water prohibitions of which mine was but a logical extension. Blacksmiths, for example, cannot draw water with other Dowayos; they must be offered water by others. Ordinary Dowayos cannot drink mountain Dowayo water unless offered it by the owners. Rainchiefs cannot drink rainwater. It is part of a system of regulated exchange that governs the passage of women, food, water between the three groups. Since I did not exchange food or women with other groups, it was appropriate that I should have my own restrictions on water. Other Dowayos would never touch my water unless I literally put it in their hands, believing that a disease would result from uninvited drinking.

The walk of some nine kilometres on a rocky road was generally an enjoyable relief from sloshing around the muddy fields. After a couple of months of this, my feet and ankles were rich in all manner of noxious fungi that blandly ignored any of the remedies I had brought with me. Trousers had a life of about a month in the rains. After that they literally rotted away from the bottoms. Wearing shorts was the obvious solution but these made my assistant instantly sullen on the grounds that men of standing did not wear them; moreover, they offered no protection from thorns, razor grass or stinging reeds with which the bush was dotted.

Once in town, I would install myself in the bar with all the other inveterate mail watchers. Sometimes there was beer to help pass the time as we sat and waited for the sound of the mail truck. Sometimes I would visit the market, a miserable group of old men and women selling a handful of peppers or strings of beads. I cannot believe that this was an economically viable occupation and was surely undertaken solely to relieve boredom. At the other end of town was a butcher who, two days a week, had meat. Since the big men of the town had reserved the major part for themselves in advance, all that was available for others was feet and intestines that were divided up with an axe. The quantity that one got for a fixed price varied capriciously since no scales were used. In and out of all this wandered the various functionaries, locals in various degrees of vagabondage, gendarmes holding hands and everywhere – children.

Through my Friday mail run, I became acquainted with a number of the teachers in particular. One notable figure was Alphonse. Alphonse was a huge Southerner who had been posted as primary school teacher out in the bush beyond the River Faro. This part of Cameroon is so remote that it is virtually part of Nigeria. Nigerian money and goods are found rather than Cameroonian and a good deal of smuggling goes on. There Alphonse lived in total isolation among the Tchamba. A friend who visited him reported that his hut was minute and his only possessions were one pair of shorts and two sandals of different colour. There was no beer. At the beginning of the dry season a small cloud of dust would appear on the horizon on the road from Tchamba. Gradually, a small dot would become visible. It would be Alphonse walking, stumbling, crawling towards Poli, crying 'Beer! Beer!' He would install himself in the bar and proceed to spend his accumulated salary on beer. It is a strong argument for the existence of a beneficent deity that he never arrived during one of the lengthy spells when there was no beer. By about four in the afternoon, Alphonse would have reached the stage where he wanted to dance.

He was a large man, gentle if unopposed, but prodigious in his furies. The tapster, often the truant pupil of one of the local teachers, would be dispatched to fetch his radio. As soon as the music started, Alphonse began to heave, like some great phenomenon of nature. Oblivious to the world, he shuffled, emitting low moans, drawing great draughts from his bottle, hips swaying, groin gyrating, head drooping. This would continue for hours until he reached a more advanced stage where everyone else had to dance as well lest he take offence. It was a matter of some concern whether the mail would arrive before Alphonse attained the point of social dancing. Alphonse was no respecter of persons and the bar would often contain nervously circling tax inspectors and gendarmes all dancing under his imperial sway, as he sighed and smiled happily in one corner.

His chief ally and fellow hell-raiser was another Southerner, Augustin. Augustin had defected from the life of a chartered accountant in the capital and become a teacher of French. He was another rugged individualist in a state that treasured fawning conformity, the only man I knew who refused to buy a membership card for the single political party. A feud had begun between himself and the local *sous-préfet*; both were notorious for their uxoriousness. It was confidently predicted among the local functionaries that one day he would 'disappear' either through some political offence or because of his activities among the wives of the Poli Fulanis. Under the influence of drink he roared round the town on a large motorbike to the great terror of young and old alike, frequently falling off, but never suffering more than superficial damage. An atmosphere of imminent disaster surrounded Augustin; wherever he went there was trouble. On one occasion when he visited me in my village he blatantly engaged in fornication with a local married woman. Dowayos expect married women to indulge in adultery and regard the seduction of each others' wives as an amusing sport. Augustin, however, had copulated with her in the husband's own hut, a serious affront. The husband soon found out, and with the logic of group responsibility, decided that I must pay him compensation. I discussed this with the Chief and other 'legal advisers' and politely refused. The husband appeared outside my hut with his brothers. He would seize Augustin the next time he came to see me. Worse still, he would beat on his motorbike with sticks. It seemed politic at this point to warn Augustin not to come out to the village for a while. True to his nature, he appeared the next day; he even parked his motorbike in front of the wronged husband's house. I was seriously concerned that there might be violence or that my relationship with the Dowayos would be jeopardized.

The husband, in fact, appeared with his brothers. Augustin produced beer he had brought from town. We all drank in silence. Several more beers were produced and Zuuldibo, with his incredible drink-scenting abilities, materialized at once. My assistant hovered nervously in the background. I distributed tobacco. Suddenly the husband, who had sat brooding in the sort

71

of smouldering silence one associates with drunken Glaswegians, began to sing a thin, tuneless song. Immediately all the other men joined in with gusto. The husband left. It is the anthropologist's role to be the earnest drone who goes round afterwards asking to have the joke explained to him, so I began asking about what I had witnessed. The words of the song were, 'Oh who would copulate with a bitter vagina?' sung in mockery of women. It seemed that the husband, lulled by the beer, had decided that all-male solidarity was more important than the fidelity of a mere wife. The matter was never alluded to again. Moreover, Zuuldibo and Augustin became the firmest of friends and shared many drinking bouts together.

Often both Alphonse and Augustin would be at the bar awaiting their salaries with all the pointless anxiety of expectant fathers. There were always huge disputes about the calculation of income tax. I noted with interest that Cameroonian school-teachers received almost the same salary in Poli as I did in London. They also received free air tickets for internal travel which they mostly sold on the black market, unless the functionaries cheated them out of them. Actually getting one's hands on the mail was a nostalgic return to the jostling bureaucracy. It was necessary to queue endlessly while all manner of details were noted minutely in school exercise books with much careful ruling of lines and precision rubber stamping. Identity papers were examined at great length. A skilled clerk could make the delivering up of a single letter last ten minutes.

Then would come the post-mortem. Those with no mail would retire to the bar to grieve. Those with mail would normally end up at the same place to celebrate. Since it was dark before seven, I almost invariably ended up trudging back to Kongle in the dark. In England one forgets how dark nights can be since we are seldom far away from some form of lighting; in Dowayoland they were pitch black and everyone carried a torch as an absolute necessity. Dowayos refuse to go beyond the boundary fence at night; darkness terrifies them. People huddle together in the smoky glow of campfires until the light returns. Outside are wild beasts, sorcery, the giant 'Pimento-head' who rains blows on unwary travellers and strikes them dumb.

72

They were truly amazed that I would roam the bush in the dark, regarding it as an act of foolhardy bravery. That I would do so alone was the act of a madman. In fact I never felt safer than in the deserted bush at night. The air would cool to the temperature of an English summer's night, generally the rain would ease off though lightning flickered silently over the high mountains. The constellations were new and splendid. Often the moon would rise later and make the scene as light as day. There were no really dangerous large predators in the area; the chief risk was treading on snakes. There was a peace and tranquillity that were far removed from the turmoil of a village and a blessed relief from trying to make sense of the Dowayos, from being stared at and pointed at, shouted at and interrogated. One's essential privacy, the first casualty of African life, was magically restored. I always arrived back from my nocturnal treks refreshed.

Very occasionally I would meet people, often rushing headlong in groups to escape from the terrors of the night, visitors having incautiously tarried in mountain villages, men returning from festivals. Sometimes they simply turned tail and bolted at the mere sight of me. The next day, there would be much amusement as they told their tale of meeting Pimento-head but having escaped from his clutches; everyone was careful to avoid the conclusion that the considerable increase in the frequency of Pimento-head sightings was largely due to my efforts. They considered that the fear of the giant was a healthy preventative of 'wandering about' in women. 'Wandering about' implied adulterous liaisons. There were even herbal charms that turned into Pimento-head that the men placed at the crossroads for this purpose. It did no harm to give the women a fright.

Gradually, as I pieced together the relations between rainchiefs, ordinary Dowayos and blacksmiths, I also formed a picture of the relations between men and women. For the physical details I relied on what close contacts, my assistant, men from the village, could be lured into revealing at the swimming place. This was lavishly supplemented by Augustin's own considerable fieldwork among pagan women. Once I had suggested one or two themes to bear in mind, he proved a rich source of information on sexual mores. He was able to confirm the odd mixture of wantonness and prudery in sexual matters exhibited by Dowayos.

Dowayos are sexually active from a relatively early age. Since Dowayos do not know how old they are one has to estimate such things, but they seem to begin their explorations about the age of eight. Sexual activity is not discouraged. A boy will be allowed to spend the night with a girl of his choice in her hut, though the mother will be expected to keep an eye on things and wanton promiscuity is not approved. Sexual relations take a turn for the worse at puberty. Premarital pregnancy carries no stigma, indeed it is taken as a welcome sign that a girl is fertile, but menstruation carries the risk of imbecility if a male comes into contact with it. A further complication is circumcision. This can happen at any age from ten to about twenty, all local boys being cut at the same time. A man may marry before he is circumcised and even have children; it is not unknown for a father to be circumcised alongside his son, though this is rare. But uncircumcised males carry a taint of femininity. They are accused of emitting the stench of women, the result of their dirty foreskins; they cannot participate in all male events; they are buried with women. Worst of all they cannot swear on their knives. The strongest oath in Dowayoland is '*Dang mi gere*', 'behold my knife'. The reference is to the knife of circumcision, a powerful object that has the power to slay witches and would certainly kill a woman. If a man uses this oath to a woman, he is very angry and she is risking a beating. Uncircumcised males who use it are mocked mercilessly and beaten if they persist; it was considered hilarious whenever I did it.

The Dowayo form of circumcision is very severe, the entire penis being peeled for its whole length. Nowadays some boys undergo the operation at the hospital but this is considered scandalous by conservative Dowayos on the grounds that not enough is removed and the boy is not isolated completely from women for up to nine months. The operation converts the imperfect being of natural birth, via a process of death and rebirth, into a wholly male person. It was made clear to me, on payment of six bottles of beer to the circumciser, that I was 'honorary circumcised'. I considered it a cheap price for exemption.

Women are not supposed to know about circumcision. They are told that it involves an operation to seal the anus with a piece of cattle-hide. This necessitates all manner of fictions. In the dry season all vegetation shrivels up in the arid heat and there is very little cover. Dowayoland is full of males walking around staring airily into space, desperately containing themselves until the coast is clear so that they can dive behind a rock to relieve themselves. In fact, women know full well what goes on, but must not publicly admit so. I considered it one of the marks of my anomalous status as a largely asexual being that women would admit this to me. It was a long time before anyone bothered to tell me about this division of knowledge. I had merely assumed that women knew about circumcision but that it was shocking to talk about it before them. There are all sorts of subjects relating to 'men's secrets' that must not be mentioned before women – ceremonies, songs, objects. In practice, it usually turned out that women knew a lot about what happened but had often not perceived the full picture. While they knew that the penis was involved in circumcision, they did not know that the whole ritual that boys go through during this operation is virtually identical with that undergone by the widows of the dead at the festivals held some years after the deaths of rich men. Thus it was unlikely that they knew that the whole skull festival was modelled on the boys' ritual at circumcision. The complete model of the culture was available to men only, as I discovered later.

It has been pointed out that women are strangely absent from anthropologists' descriptions. They are supposed to be difficult, ill-informed sources of knowledge. In my own case, I found them extremely helpful – after an unfortunate start.

As usual the problem was one of language. I wanted to talk to an old woman about changes in Dowayo behaviour over the years, and thought it wise to ask her husband for permission beforehand. 'But what do you want to talk to her about?' he asked. 'I want to find out about marriage,' I said. 'I want to talk about customs, about adultery, about . . .' There was a gasp of horror and disbelief from both husband and assistant. I swiftly ran a mental check on the tones I had used but could find nothing wrong. I went into a huddle with Matthieu. The problem lay in a

Dowayo idiom. In Dowayo, one does not 'perform' a custom, one 'speaks' it. Likewise, one does not 'commit' adultery, one 'speaks' it. I had therefore announced my intention of performing rituals with the man's wife and committing adultery with her.

Once that misunderstanding had been cleared up, I found her a most useful informant. Whereas men regarded themselves as the repositories of the ultimate secrets of the universe and had to be cajoled into sharing them with me, women knew that any information available to them was unimportant and could quite happily be repeated to an outsider. They often opened up new fields of inquiry for me by alluding in passing to some belief or ceremony I had never heard of, that the men would have been reluctant to mention.

Male and female lives remain largely separate. A man may have a large number of wives but he spends his time with his male friends and she spends her time with co-wives or female neighbours. The pattern is broadly similar to that in the North of England. A woman prepares food for her husband and children but he eats separately from her, possibly with an elder son. They cultivate separately. She grows her food, he his, although he may help with certain of the harder parts of the agricultural cycle. They meet for sexual purposes in his hut in accordance with a rota worked out in advance between the wives. There is little familiarity or affection by Western standards. Dowayos told me with wonder about an American missionary in Dowayoland whose wife would run from the house to greet him when he returned from a trip. They cackled with amazed amusement at Dowayos having to ask the missionary's wife for lifts instead of the husband, and at the way he never seemed to beat her.

It should not be assumed from this that Dowayo wives are poor, browbeaten shrinking violets. They give as good as they get, and stick up for themselves with a will. Their ultimate sanction is simply to walk out and return to their parents' village. The husband knows that in these circumstances he will have great difficulty in gaining the return of the cattle he has paid for the woman. He may well end up with neither woman nor cattle. For this reason, he will delay the actual transfer of cattle as long as possible. Wives desert their husbands not infrequently and the system of cattle transfer in Dowayoland is every bit as much subject to delay as the most efficient Cameroonian bank. The frequency of marital breakdown and the failure of many husbands to ever finish payments for wives can enrage the ethnographic inquirer as he finds the same woman being entered two or three times in his calculations. Thus a woman may leave her husband for another and each man will placidly inform the anthropologist that she is his wife. The first husband is quite willing to say how much he paid for the woman but omits to mention that the cattle of brideprice were never delivered. The second husband indicates the price he paid for the woman but forgets to say that he paid this to her wronged first husband, not to her parents. By now, the first husband may well have used the cattle to repay other debts in women – long overdue. The parents of the erring wife now go to the second husband to try to make him pay up the cattle that the first never delivered, threatening to take the woman away. He ripostes by mentioning an unliquidated debt three generations back where one of *his* female relatives was not paid for. A hopelessly convoluted lawsuit ensues.

Dowayos never justify their choice of a wife in terms of beauty, but rather with references to her being obedient and good-natured. A woman must never see a penis after circumcision or she would become ill. A man should never see a vagina or he would lose all sexual desire. Hence the sexual act is a rather furtive affair conducted in total darkness, with neither party naked. The woman does not remove the bunch of leaves she wears fore and aft. In former times, men wore a loin-cloth that would be unfastened to allow removal of the gourd penis-sheath that was required for the circumcised. Nowadays shorts are the fashion and only old men or those engaged in ritual activity wear sheaths. As a joke, women make with their cheeks the plopping sound of a male privy member being removed from a sheath; this sound also serves as a coy euphemism for the sexual act itself. Women always expect to receive reward for sexual services even within marriage, a fact that has led to uncharitable comparisons between their conception of marriage and prostitution by mission preachers; there is always a strong sense of keeping of accounts even between husband and wife. Such information was built up piecemeal; my research into the festivals that stand apart from everyday life was quite different.

By sheer good fortune I had appeared in Dowayoland in a year following a good millet harvest (Dowayo years run from one millet harvest in early November to the next); many had taken advantage of this abundance to organize skull festivals for their dead.

At death a Dowayo body is wrapped in burial cloth made from local cotton and the skins of cattle that are slaughtered for the occasion. It is buried in a crouching position. Some two weeks later, the head is removed via a weak spot left in the wrapping for this purpose. It is examined for witchcraft and placed in a pot in a tree. Thereafter male and female (or uncircumcised) skulls are treated differently. Male skulls are placed out in the bush behind the hut where the skulls find their final rest. Female skulls are placed behind a hut in the village where the woman was born: on marriage a woman moves to her husband's village; at death she moves back.

After several years the spirits of the dead may begin to plague their living kinsmen, visiting them in dreams, causing illness, disdaining to enter the wombs of women so that children can be born and the spirit reincarnated. This is the sign that it is high time to organize a skull festival. Normally, a rich man will begin by soliciting the support of his kinsmen and offering them beer. If two beer parties pass without dissent, the affair is arranged. Dowayos become very fractious when in drink and it is unusual for a really drunken occasion to pass without dispute, requiring positive effort on the part of all present. The fact that two parties are not marred by fighting can be held to indicate a singular sense of common purpose.

I had heard through Zuuldibo that such a festival was to be held in a village some fifteen miles away and conducted a preliminary foray to establish the truth of it.

The timing of events in Dowayoland is a nightmare to anyone seeking to plan more than ten minutes in the future. Time is measured in months, weeks and days. The older Dowayos have only the vaguest notion of what makes up a week; it seems that the notion is to be viewed as a cultural borrowing like names for the months. Old people reckon in days from the present; there is complicated terminology for points in the past and future such as 'the day before the day before yesterday'. With such a system, it is virtually impossible to fix precisely a day when something is going to happen. Added to this is the fact that Dowayos are firmly independent and resent bitterly anyone trying to organize them. They do things in their own good time. This took me a long while to get used to; I hated wasting time, resented losing it and expected return for spending it. I felt that I must hold the world record for hearing 'It is not the right time for that', whenever I sought to pin down Dowayos to show me a particular thing at a particular time. Arrangements to meet at a fixed time or place never worked. People were astonished that I should be offended when they turned up a day or even a week late, or when I walked ten miles to find they were not at home. Time was simply not something that could be allocated. Other more material things fell into the same category. Tobacco, for example, admitted no firm drawing of lines between mine and thine. I was initially disconcerted by my assistant helping himself to my tobacco stock without so much as a by-your-leave, though he would never dream of touching my water. Tobacco, like time, is an area where the degree of flexibility permitted by the culture is grossly at variance with our own. It is not permissible to retain possession of tobacco; friends have the right to go through your pockets and take it. Whenever I paid informants with a bag of tobacco, they would swiftly hide it about their person with blatant disregard for the rules of modesty and scuttle off home desperately worried lest they encounter anyone *en route* to their hiding place.

This outing was my first visit to the valley known as the Valley of Borassa Palms on account of the numerous examples of this species that flourish only here. On old maps the road is still shown as running through the valley, but it has now fallen into considerable disrepair. Nevertheless, by careful driving it was possible to penetrate several kilometres into the brooding valley with its great vista of the mountains that mark the border with Nigeria. The villages here were much closer to the traditional mountain Dowayo type than in my own area. It was also impossible to understand a word anyone said, the tones being somewhat different, having been exaggerated into huge swoops and leaps. After a couple of hours on the road with Matthieu and Zuuldibo sailing on ahead, we arrived at the compound of the Chief of the area. The huts were so close together, for defensive purposes, that one had to get down on hands and knees to wriggle between them. The entrance huts were so low that we all had to get on our bellies and crawl to get in at all. In Kongle, the average height for a man is about five feet six or less. Here, there were husky six-footers, who must have found these arrangements a considerable inconvenience.

We were received with great ceremony by the Chief, an astonishing old pirate with one eye and decorative scars cut deep all over his face. There was beer about and Zuuldibo began attacking it with a vengeance. I began to fear that we would spend all day here. It was confirmed that the skull festival would occur; the exact date remained a little hazy. It was not until we were doing the 'day after the day after . . .' business that I realized the Chief was drunk. Zuuldibo was making great strides to catch him up. He spoke Dowayo, the other Fulani. One of his sons joined us and spoke French. After some time it became clear that he had no idea who I was, having taken me for the Dutch linguist some thirty years my senior who had lived in his village for years and only recently left. It seems all white men looked the same to him. He would be delighted to have me attend whenever the ceremony happened. He would send me word. I knew from experience that he would not, but thanked him heartily and managed to lure Zuuldibo away by making my water bottle available to carry enough beer to see him through the journey.

It was by now late afternoon on a very hot day and the skin was coming off my face in handfuls. Dowayos observed this closely, doubtless hoping that my true black nature would soon start showing through. Even aged Dowayos trip along at about twice the European walking speed, leaping from rock to rock like goats and I began to regret the lack of water. My entourage bore with me kindly, being amazed that any white man should be able to walk at all. They all had inflated notions of our helplessness, susceptibility to illness or discomfort which were explained by the fact that we had 'supple skin'. It is a fact that the skin on the feet and elbows of Africans is inch-thick, horny hide that enables them to walk over sharp rocks or even glass, barefoot, without risk. Finally we reached the car and set off, giving a lift to a passing woman. Scarce had we travelled a mile before she vomited, in typical fashion, all over me. While I was in Dowayoland, many people and dogs availed themselves of the opportunity to vomit over me. In the wet season there was no problem; you pulled up at a river and jumped in fully clothed, to wash it off.

Back at the village, I was pleasantly surprised at my assistant's native wit. Seeing the way things were going in the drunken Chief's compound, he had slipped away and sought out a young lady of his acquaintance, who would be engaged in preparing the beer for the festival. From its state of fermentation, he inferred that it would be ready in two days and sour in four. This fixed the date. This initiative coinciding with pay day, we were both somewhat surprised when I gave him a small bonus. The incident marked a turning point in our relations and he became suddenly assiduous in ferreting out information and festivals. As he left, he pointed out that the trip had been unnecessary, since one would be able to tell by the number of people passing through the village when the ceremony would be held. Moreover, there was no need to ask permission to attend. Festivals were public affairs; the greater the number of outsiders, the greater the success.

The day of the festival dawned bright and sunny. I woke to the normal sounds of Dowayos standing outside my hut saying to Matthieu, 'Is he *still* in bed?' 'Hasn't he got up yet?' It was a quarter to six. This was the first opportunity to test my equipment – cameras and tape-recorder – in the field. I had shown Matthieu how to operate the recorder and we had agreed that he would be in charge of that while I concentrated on photographs and notes. This pleased him greatly and he strutted around pushing people out of his way and making sure that everyone was aware of his onerous responsibilities. One of the bridges had washed away in the interim and another five kilometres were added to the journey on foot. Particularly unpleasant was the crossing of a raging torrent, slipping on the wet rocks and trying to hold equipment over our heads. Matthieu, being a plains Dowayo, fared about as badly as I did, while our escort, a montagnard of about fifty,

81

shepherded us carefully across, clinging to the rocks with his bare feet.

Bands of people were teeming over the bush on small paths, all converging on the festival. The women had relinquished their customary leaves for strips of cloth, a sure sign that this was a public occasion. By law, Dowayos have to wear clothes and it is forbidden to take photographs of bare female breasts. If strictly observed, this would make photography impossible and so, like most others, I disregarded this regulation, uncomfortably aware that it might cause trouble if the gendarmes had turned up. When we reached the village we were overwhelmed by the number of strangers to be greeted. A swarm of grinning children followed us, giggling and wrestling in the mud, doddering old men shook hands with us, obliging youths offered to let me listen to their radios so I would not be deprived of constant Nigerian music. Patiently, I tried to explain that what I really wanted was Dowayo music. The old men were pleased, the younger baffled.

An enormous crowd had gathered in the cattle park, ankle deep in mud. Zuuldibo was already installed on a grass mat, resplendent in sunglasses and a sword. We drank beer and he tried to explain what was going on.

There were always numerous problems with Dowayo 'explanations'. Firstly, they missed out the essential piece of information that made things comprehensible. No one told me that this village was where the Master of the Earth, the man who controlled the fertility of all plants, lived, and that consequently various parts of the ceremony would be different from elsewhere. This is fair enough; some things are too obvious to mention. If we were explaining to a Dowayo how to drive a car, we should tell him all sorts of things about gears and road signs before mentioning that one tried not to hit other cars.

Dowayo explanations always ended up in a circle I came to know well. 'Why do you do this?' I would ask.

'Because it is good.'

'Why is it good?'

'Because the ancestors told us to.'

(Slyly) 'Why did the ancestors tell you to?'

'Because it is good.'

I could never find a way round 'the ancestors' with whom all explanation began and ended.

Dowayos baffled me at first by the way in which they used their categories prescriptively. 'Who organized this festival?' I would ask.

'The man with the porcupine quills in his hair.'

'I can't see anyone with porcupine quills in his hair.'

'No, he's not wearing them.'

Things were always described as they should be, not as they were.

Then, again, Dowayos are addicted to joking. I always made a point of noting what special leaves various participants were wearing at festivals since it seemed reasonable that their special costumes might be important. I was constantly deceived by 'jokers', males circumcised at the same time as a man or females who began to menstruate at the same time as a woman. They would turn up in a bizarre collection of weird leaves and disrupt matters generally. It was important to identify them at the start lest their particular absurdities be considered part of the standard practice they were subverting.

It was also important to realize that the same person might be active at a festival in several different capacities. At this particular event one of the clowns, who alone may handle the skulls, was also younger brother of the dead man for whom the whole thing had been organized. He would therefore alternate between being a clown and being an organizer and it was far from clear to an outsider where one began and the other ended. He was also doing many of the jobs normally performed by a skull-house sorcerer on the grounds of the extraordinary infirmity of the latter. So he was one man but occupied three separate positions in the cultural system.

All this, naturally, was way above any level of analysis of which I was capable at that time. I merely sat on a wet rock, watched, asked idiot questions and took photographs of the parts that seemed interesting.

That first day, apart from the clowns, there was much to see. The clowns were extravagant, their faces painted half white, half black. They wore rubbish or old rags and spoke in a high-pitched scream partly in Fulani, partly in Dowayo, shouting out obscenities and nonsense. 'The cunt of the beer!' they screamed. The crowd roared with pleasure. They exposed themselves, produced ear-shattering farts by what mechanism I know not. They attempted to copulate with each other. They were delighted with me. They 'took photographs' through a broken bowl, 'wrote notes' on banana leaves. I managed to give as good as I got; when they asked for money, I solemnly handed them a bottle-top.

Just outside the village were the skulls of the dead, male and female segregated. Goats, cattle and sheep had been slain in large numbers and their excrement flung on the skulls. The organizers lopped the heads off chickens and spattered their blood on the deceased. The clowns immediately began to fight for possession of the carcasses, stamping around in the mess of mud, blood and excrement. The heat was intense, the crowd enormous. It was considered amusing by the clowns to seek to splash those present with as much blood and filth as possible. The stench was terrible, and several Dowayos began to vomit, thereby adding to the miasma. I removed myself out of range. A torrential downpour began, and Zuuldibo and I huddled miserably under a tree, holding palm-leaves over our heads.

There was a murmuring in the crowd and it became clear that a little old man was the centre of interest. He was small and wiry, mouth set in a firm rictus, the result, as I later discovered, of a second-hand set of false teeth. To see him remove these was apparently one of the wonders of Dowayoland. He sat bolt upright under a red umbrella, looking to the right and the left with an expression of benign omniscience. No one would tell me who he was. 'An old man known for his goodness,' Zuuldibo explained. 'I don't know,' said Matthieu, looking furtive. The old man was brought a large jar of beer which he tasted and then disappeared into the bush. There was tension in the air. No one spoke. After some ten minutes the old man reappeared. The rain began to ease off. A general sigh of relief was obvious even to me. I had no idea what was afoot but knew better than to press for an explanation; perhaps Zuuldibo would be more forthcoming in private.

There now followed one of those considerable longueurs that characterized all organized Dowayo activity. I found myself able to drop into 'fieldwork gear', a state almost of suspended animation where one is able to wait for hours without impatience, frustration or expectation of anything better. After a long time it became clear that nothing further could happen today. Some relatives, it seemed, had misunderstood the date of the festival and not turned up. Perhaps they would come tomorrow. There began a fervent arranging of accommodation. Matthieu went away to arrange my own lodging. Zuuldibo announced he would sleep under a tree as long as there was beer.

A short trek through the bush, across two rivers and through stinging reeds, brought me to my own rest in the hut of an ingratiating man, who expelled his son so that he himself would have a roof for the night. Upon my inquiry, the man gave me to understand that his son would receive the sexual favours of a Dowayo maid that night and so not be the worse for it.

The hut was the most squalid I'd yet seen. A box in the corner contained a selection of rotting chicken carcasses, an indication presumably that the man had offered their blood to the ancestors that day. In the roof beams were various artefacts for use at later stages of the festival: the flutes played when a man has been slain, the horse tails and burial cloth that are used to ornament the skulls before a man dances with them. The floor was covered with filth. The bed, when I settled into it, proved to contain several half-gnawed hunks of meat and bones, remnants of sacrificed cattle.

Away in the main village, there was drumming and singing and the rhythmic rise and fall lulled me to sleep, curled up under my own wet clothes. A scratching at the door roused me; I had momentary fears of another Coo-ee lady, but it was only Matthieu bringing me hot water in a seething calabash. 'It's boiled for five minute, *patron*, safe to drink.' I had concealed a mixture of instant milk and coffee about my person, with copious sugar for any Dowayo who might want it. We split the coffee between us, Matthieu adding six spoons of sugar to his own. Rousing myself to a sense of duty, I asked about various of the articles in the roof and received enlightenment. 'The old man, today, is the

Old Man of Kpan, head of all the rainmakers. Zuuldibo will introduce you tomorrow.' He left and I heard a Dowayo say loudly, 'Is your *patron* asleep *already*?'

The first man I saw the next day was Augustin, out for a break from the rigours of Poli. Like all good urban Africans, he would never entertain the thought of walking anywhere. He had managed to bring his motorbike all the way, had arrived late and spent the night with yet another obliging Dowayo woman who turned out to be a wayward wife of the Old Man of Kpan. It appeared that this was her native village and she had returned for the festival. Her brother had shown Augustin the door in no uncertain terms with dire threats that if the rainchief found out about this they would all be struck by lightning. My mental dossier on him, opened only the day before, was filling up fast.

The events of the day drove him from my mind. A Dowayo skull festival is a bit like a Russian circus, with four different things happening at once. After a final bout of excrement-throwing, the clowns began to clean the skulls. Meanwhile, girls originating from the village had been returned by their husbands and decorated as Fulani warriors. They danced on a hill, waving spears to the accompaniment of 'talking' flutes that speak by imitating the tones of the language. This is yet another aspect of the Dowayo tongue I never mastered. The flutes encouraged them to display the wealth of their husbands, who harried them mercilessly to put on a good show, tricking them out in sunglasses, borrowed watches, radios and other consumer goods, in addition to their robes. Some men pinned money to their heads.

In another part of the village were the widows of the men whose festival this was. They were decked in long leaf skirts with conical hats of the same vegetation on their heads, dancing in long lines like chorus girls. At the time I could only record as much information as possible, leaving any attempt at intelligent analysis to another time. Matthieu flitted from one group to another, recording as much of the material as he could, shoving his way to the front of every crowd in a way that I could never have done.

In the distance, yet another group appeared carrying a strange bundle and waving knives. Later, I found out that these were the circumcised carrying the bow of the man whose festival this was and singing circumcision songs. Suddenly, a group of boys rushed out screaming at them. I thought I was witnessing a genuine spontaneous brawl but from the enjoyment of spectators it became clear that this was a standard element. 'The uncircumcised,' explained a helpful man beside me. 'Always, thus.' I could not resist asking why. He stared at me as if I was a fool. 'The ancestors told us to.' He moved away.

Something was going on at the skulls and I dashed back, while Matthieu kept his eye on the battle between the two groups. The skulls of the men were being wrapped, with the argument that inevitably accompanied co-operative endeavour in Dowayoland, in what even I could recognize as the dress of a circumcision candidate. The skulls of women were ignominiously dumped on one side and forgotten. All women and children were chased away. The skulls of the men were jostled and the flutes I had seen in my roof were blown. 'They are threatening the dead with circumcision,' Zuuldibo explained enigmatically. A man hefted them on his head and a strange, haunting melody was struck up with odd, booming gongs, drums and deep flutes. Long trains of burial cloth were strung out from the bundle and supported by swaying men, so that it resembled nothing so much as a great spider. Others put on the bloody skins of the cattle slaughtered for the occasion, the heads resting against their own, a strip of raw flesh gripped in their teeth, and circled the skulls with an odd stamping motion, bowing and swerving. All was stink, noise and motion. At the entrance to the village, the widows danced and beckoned in the dead who moved slowly round the central tree before being placed where the skulls of slaughtered cattle are exhibited over a gateway. A man leapt up beside them, the organizer of the festival, and shouted: 'It is thanks to me that these men were circumcised. If it were not for the white man, I would have killed a man.'

At the time, of course, I took this to be an allusion to myself, imagining that all manner of obscene happenings had been suppressed on my account alone. My first reaction was one of disappointment. 'Don't mind me,' I would have shouted, 'that's what I came for!' Subsequent inquiry revealed that in the old days a man had indeed been slain for such festivals and his skull pounded to pieces with a rock, but that the central government – French, German and Cameroonian – had put a stop to this.

The occasion now degenerated into a mere beer-drinking and general dance and we decided to head back to Kongle. On the way, Zuuldibo made a detour and led us out to an isolated compound on the slopes of the mountains. Inside sat the Old Man of Kpan. We went through elaborate greetings. I was clutched to his heart and he went into an ecstasy of sighing, moaning and clucking like a maiden aunt over a favourite nephew. More warm beer was prepared and we sat around in the gathering gloom talking, the Old Man occasionally breaking off in mid-phrase to gasp out his delight at my presence. He understood that I was interested in the customs of the Dowayos. He had lived a long time and seen much. He would help me. I should come to his house in a short while. He would send for me. This was his busy season – he looked knowing; I tried to look knowing back. I would be the second white man to visit his valley. 'Was the first French or German?' I asked, trying to fix the period. 'No, no, a white man like yourself.' I handed round some cola nuts I had with me and we took our leave, picking our way through the granite boulders and waterlogged paths down to the main track. Thick mist was beginning to build up in the valley bottoms and the night was going to be very cold indeed. We were all shivering by the time we reached the car, and looking forward to fleeing to the comforts of Kongle. Weather is essentially local in West Africa; rainfall in one spot may be twice as hard a few miles away. Kongle was always ten degrees warmer than this end of Dowayoland at night; round the other side of the mountain was hotter still.

As soon as the car came in sight, it was clear that something was very wrong. It appeared to be at a strange angle. In the whole time I was in Dowayoland the only time anyone ever stole from me was at the mission, and so I had acquired the habit of leaving everything unlocked when away from civilizing influences. Perhaps someone had released the brake and moved it?

A moment's inspection revealed all. I had parked on the edge of a ravine, the road in front leading down to the washed-out bridge. The torrential downpour of the previous day had softened the edge sufficiently for the weight of the car to cause it to crumble. It was now perched with the wheels of one side over a sixty-foot drop, so perfectly balanced that it swayed slightly to the touch. It was a situation where brute physical force was required, and everyone was still at the festival. There was nothing else for it. Clutching notebooks, camera and recorder, we all turned around and trudged dispiritedly back. It was a miserable end to a good day. Zuuldibo further depressed us by insisting on making statements such as 'It is man's place to suffer.' These had clearly been acquired from local Muslims as one of the comforts of their religion. He had a seemingly inexhaustible stock of such platitudes. 'Man proposes, God disposes,' he intoned as we wallowed in the icy river. 'No man may know the future,' he declaimed, crawling on all fours up to the village.

We then searched for the local chief. If there is one thing less profitable than trying to fix the time of a meeting with Dowayos, it is trying to find a person or place. The Chief was variously reported, with complete confidence, to be in his hut, in Poli, ill, drunk – everything but dead and in France. I never established to my satisfaction whether this reflected a basic epistemological difference between us – unlike notions of 'knowledge', 'truth', 'evidence' – or whether they were simply telling lies. Were they telling me what they thought I would wish to hear? Did they hold that firmly believed error was better than doubt? Was it simply a cultural rule that you tried to confuse outsiders as much as possible? I inclined towards the last view.

Finally he was located and went into loud lamentations over our misfortune. Nothing could be done at night, he explained, because of the dangers of the dark, but tomorrow morning he himself would organize the affair. 'It is a man's place to suffer,' I said. Zuuldibo giggled.

Matthieu and I shared a hut in the middle of a banana plantation, feeding off the produce, in the bitter cold. The hut was provided with the remains of a fire and a sleeping dog who ignored us. I realize now that it must have been someone's cooking hut, but why it was out there in isolation remains a mystery. Moreover, no sane Dowayo would ever allow a dog to lie inside a hut by the fire. Matthieu, indeed, reacted in true Dowayo fashion and began looking for a log to beat the dog on the head. When he found one I pre-empted him by putting it on the fire. We spent the night lying on the beaten dirt floor in our wet clothes. I had the better of it since the dog adopted my feet as its resting place, but it will not be remembered as my most cheery night in Dowayoland. The cold was intense, Matthieu snored, the dog had a cough. I tried to calculate the odds of the car I had not yet paid for toppling over the cliff, comforting myself with thoughts of all the good material I had collected that day, even if I did have no idea what it was all about. Shortly before dawn I fell asleep, head on my camera case, notebooks under my hand – rather like a medieval apprentice sleeping with the tools of his trade.

Matthieu roused me at first light. The phlegmatic dog slept on. After a relatively short spell of dithering, we set off with four stalwart men towards the car. A Peugeot 404 is a very heavy car and I could not really see that four men would do much good; I had been thinking more in terms of twelve. From student debauches, I seemed to recall that it took four to move a Mini. Zuuldibo entertained us with a tale of a man suffering from diarrhoea with whom he had shared that night. Dowayo has all manner of extraordinary sounds to describe motion or smell. Zuuldibo rang the changes on all of them, so that everyone was in high spirits by the time we reached the car. Without waiting for instructions the men crawled round to the side over the ravine and, clinging with bare toes to a ledge, simply lifted the car with insulting ease and pushed it back on firm ground. Their obvious lack of effort suggested that two might have done it. Zuuldibo was ecstatic, clapping his hands and slapping his thighs. He let off another stream of tongue-trills, clicks and nasalizations to celebrate. I was embarrassed, realizing that I ought to be handing out change as a token of thanks. Alas, I had none on me and so passed out a few paltry cigarettes. The men were visibly crestfallen but made no complaint. After this I always made sure that I went on location with water, a tin of meat, small change and anti-malarial pills for a week; I had taken none for two days and began to fear the worst. I could already feel a fever developing and was anxious to get back to my kit with all speed.

A day's rest re-established our morale. The only lasting damage seemed to be my feet. Strange blotches of blood had appeared around the nails of my big toes accompanied by intense itching. I had jiggers. These are unpleasant burrowing parasites that lay eggs in the living flesh until the whole foot is rotten with them. Old Africa hands will tell you to place yourself firmly in the care of the locals who have ways of digging them out with a safety-pin without bursting the egg-sacs. Alas, Dowayos have no safety-pins and lack experience with these creatures. Having to fall back on my own resources I dug them out with a penknife, taking liberal quantities of flesh with them, to avoid eggs, and washed the wounds with alcohol and antibiotic. This drastic but necessary proceeding somewhat reduced my mobility for a while, but that was relatively unimportant. At last I had material to work on and began by elucidating the notes I had made at the festival. Each page of notes would keep me occupied for several days, checking what it was that I had seen, how it compared with the festival in my own village, what other cultural knowledge it implied. For example, the man who carried the skulls at the dance was not just anyone, he had to be in a *duuse* relationship with the dead man. To understand what this word implied, I had to sort out all the kinship terms. Trying to do this even roughly with French equivalents is quite impossible, but the mistakes Dowayos make when speaking French are very helpful. For example, they cannot distinguish between nephew and uncle, or between grandfather and grandson. This suggested that the same terms would be used for them in Dowayo, and indeed this proved to be the case. The terminology is strongly reciprocal. If I call a man by one term, he calls me by the same term. But it took me a long time to work it all out. In the end, I collected together my last three bottles of beer – since Poli had run out, the last beer for two hundred miles – and borrowed the schoolhouse with its blackboard. The men lounging at the crossroads were only too glad to come and talk to this benevolent madman in return for the beer. They rapidly picked up the principles of kinship charts and we had a most informative session. Much has been written about primitive peoples' ability or inability to deal with hypothetical questions. I was never sure whether my difficulties with them were purely linguistic or whether much more was involved. 'If you had a sister,' I would start, 'and she married a man, what would you call ...'

'I haven't got a sister.'

'No, but if you had a sister ...'

'But I haven't got a sister. I have four brothers.'

After a number of frustrated attempts at this, Matthieu intervened. 'No, no *patron*. Like this. A man has a sister. Another man takes her. She is his wife. The man calls her husband, how?' He would get an answer. I adopted this style and had no more trouble – until we got to the term *duuse*. 'Who is your *duuse*?' I tried.

'We joke with him.'

'How do you know he is your *duuse*?'

'As children we are told. We joke with him.'

'Where does he live?'

'He can live anywhere.'

'If he is your *duuse*, what does your father call him?'

Pause. 'He will call him grandfather.'

'What does your son call him?'

'My son calls him grandfather.'

Light began to dawn.

'Do you call him grandfather?'

'Yes.'

In Dowayoland all old men are called grandfather by young men. The usage meant nothing but an age difference. I had spent most of an afternoon sorting that one out the previous day. I tried another line. 'Is your *duuse* one of your own family or a relative through marriage?' 'Own family,' said one. 'Through marriage,' said another. 'He is like a grandfather.'

I tried another tack. 'How many *duuse* do you have?'

'I cannot know.'

It occurred to me that the word might refer to other aspects of the world than biological kinship, that it might be a term of an entirely different type. I tried everything, residence, skull-house affiliation, exchange relationships, and still did not feel I knew what the term meant. I adopted another ploy of getting people to introduce me to their *duuse* and we would sit down and painfully trace the relation between them. Finally, I built up a picture of what it was. A *duuse* was someone to whom I was linked by a common relative of great-grandfather generation or beyond with at least one female linkage in between. In other words, it was someone such as my mother's grandfather, for whom no other term existed, who belonged to a different skull-house than myself and was on the very fringes where it was impossible to trace clear kinship links. This explained why, even when I got two *duuse* together, they would often give me different accounts of the links between them. A man, then, would have a great number of potential *duuse* out of which he would select a small group with whom to joke and engage in ritual activity.

Similar problems arose over the most trivial things: the feathers a man wore on different occasions, the leaves used for special rituals, the animals that might or might not be killed. All of these were potentially important for understanding what sort of a cultural world the Dowayos lived in. For example, the leopard occupies a place of great significance in their world, although there have been no leopards in Dowayoland for thirty years. Leopards are slayers of men and cattle and are equated with this aspect of Man. Circumcisers, as shedders of human blood, are required to grunt like leopards hunting, while the boys they cut dress as young leopards. If one kills a leopard, one is required to undergo the same ritual as one who has killed a man. Man-killers are referred to as 'leopards' and allowed to wear leopard-claws on their hats. When talking about their burial rites, the Dowayos made great play with the fact that the leopard, like themselves, puts the skulls of the dead in trees, a reference to its habit of dragging its prey into a tree to eat it. Powerful and dangerous men such as the rainmakers are believed to be able to turn into leopards. All these diverse attitudes come together and 'make sense' if one looks at them as a way of thinking about the wild and violent part of man's nature.

But even such a simple and – to an anthropologist – obvious area of research took weeks of sustained effort to sort out. People were reluctant to talk about rainchiefs and leopards. I only found out by chatting to a boy I bumped into while walking into town on one of my Friday mail runs. Rain trapped us under a tree and the conversation turned quite naturally to rainmakers. He pointed out to me a mountain with a permanent cloud over it. 'That's where one of them lives,' he said. 'Domboulko. Even in the dry season there's always water there. But the best is my father at Kpan. When he dies, I shall buy the secret of rain after he becomes a leopard.' I pricked up my ears and began to mine this vein of pure gold as the youth chatted on quite unconcernedly about precisely the things that interested me most. By the time we reached Poli, I knew about the importance of special mountains and caves, the existence of stones to make rain, the power of the rainmaker to kill with lightning (and the fact that he had false teeth). Once I knew about these things, it was no problem to check on them with people from my village. But that piece of the picture concerning leopards and rainchiefs had only come my way through sheer luck. If I had not been on that particular road at that particular time I might never have heard it, or only much later.

As it was, even with the most striking animals such as leopards, I had problems with informants. Popularly, Africans are supposed to be seamed with native wisdom and the folklore of plants and creatures. They are expert in identifying them from spore, scent, marks on trees. They engage in meticulous analysis of which plant a certain leaf, fruit or bark belongs to. It is their singular misfortune to be constantly interpreted by Westerners who have various axes to grind. In the days of the bland assumption of Western cultural superiority, it was intuitively obvious to all that Africans were wrong about most things and simply not too bright. It was therefore not surprising that their minds never rose higher than their bellies. The anthropologist was inevitably cast in the role of the refuter of this view of primitive man, seeking to show that there was a sense or logic in his ways and possibly a wisdom in his mind that escaped the Western observer. In these days of the New Romanticism, the ethical anthropologist is surprised to find himself suddenly on the other wing. Primitive man is used by Westerners nowadays as surely as he was by Rousseau or Montaigne to prove a point about their

own society and castigate those aspects of it they find un-
attractive. Contemporary 'thinkers' pay as little heed to fact or
balanced judgement as their forebears. An example that particularly struck me even before Dowayoland was at an exhibition
of Red Indian artefacts. A wooden canoe was displayed. 'Wooden
canoes,' we were informed, 'operate in harmony with the environment and are non-polluting.' Beside it was a picture of its
process of construction with Indians burning down large tracts
of forest to obtain the correct timber and discarding most of the
wood to rot. The 'Noble Savage' has risen from the grave, and is
alive and well and living in N.W.1 as well as some anthropology
departments.

The basic truth about Dowayos is that they knew less about
the animals of the African bush than I did. As trackers they
could tell motorbike tracks from human footprints but that was
about the pinnacle of their achievement. They believed, like most
Africans, that chameleons were poisonous. They assured me that
cobras were harmless. They did not know that caterpillars turn
into butterflies. They could not tell one bird from another or be
relied upon to identify trees accurately. Many of the plants did
not have names though they used them quite often, and reference
involved lengthy explanations: 'That plant you use to get the
bark you make the dye from.' Much of the game in Dowayoland
has been exhausted by trapping. As far as 'living in harmony
with nature' is concerned, the Dowayos are non-starters. They
reproached me often for not bringing a machine gun from the
land of the white men to enable them to finally eradicate the
pathetic clusters of antelope that still persist in their country.
When Dowayos began cultivating cotton for the government
monopoly, amounts of pesticide were made available to them.
Dowayos immediately adopted it for fishing purposes. They
would fling it into the streams to be able to recover the poisoned
fish that floated to the surface. This poison rapidly displaced the
tree-bark they had traditionally used to suffocate fish. 'It's
wonderful,' they explained. 'You throw it in and it kills everything, small fish, big fish, for miles downstream.'

Every year they start vast bushfires, quite deliberately, to speed
the growth of new grass. The resulting conflagrations involve

vast slaughter of young animals and considerable risk to human life and limb.

All these factors were involved in the simple problem of talking to Dowayos about leopards. The linguistic difficulties alone were considerable. The Dowayos have a perfectly adequate word for leopard, *naamyo*. For 'lion', however, they use the compound 'old-female-leopard'. For lesser wildcats such as the civet cat or serval, they use the compound 'sons-of-leopard'. The name for elephant is dangerously close, differing only by tone from 'lion'. To make matters worse, the first French-speaking Dowayo I asked about the terminology made a genuine mistake and gave me the word *naamyo* as meaning 'lion'. The problem of knowing, when I used the compound 'old-female-leopard', whether we were talking about lions, aged leopards of the female sex, or both at the same time, became acute. In the end I managed to lay my hands on some postcards depicting African fauna. I had at least a lion and a leopard and showed them to people to see if they could spot the difference. Alas, they could not. The reason lay not in their classifications of animals but rather in the fact that they could not identify photographs. It is a fact that we tend to forget in the West that people have to learn to be able to see photographs. We are exposed to them from birth so that, for us, there is no difficulty in identifying faces or objects from all sorts of angles, in differing light and even with distorting lenses. Dowayos have no such tradition of visual art; theirs is limited to bands of geometric designs. Nowadays, of course, Dowayo children experience images through schoolbooks or identity cards; by law, all Dowayos must carry an identity card with their photograph on it. This was always a mystery to me since many who have identity cards have never been to the city, and there is no photographer in Poli. Inspection of the cards shows that often pictures of one Dowayo served for several different people. Presumably the officials are not much better at recognizing photographs than Dowayos. When I was collecting vocabulary of several obvious areas such as names of the parts of the body, I drew an outline of a man and a woman with somewhat hazy pudenda so that they could point to areas that bore a single name. This drawing was considered a major wonder and for months afterwards men would come to my hut to ask to see it. (They were particularly anxious about whether I had depicted the penis in its full circumcised glory – in which case they would have asked me not to show it to women.) The point was that men could not tell the difference between the male and the female outlines. I put this down simply to my bad drawing, until I tried using photographs of lions and leopards. Old men would stare at the cards, which were perfectly clear, turn them in all manner of directions, and then say something like 'I do not know this man.' Children could identify the animals but were totally ignorant of their ritual importance. In the end I made a trip to Garoua. There, in the market, is a stall bearing the splendid title 'Syndicate of traditional healers'. Here are to be found many weird and wonderful things, parts of plants, leopards' claws, bats' eyes, hyenas' anuses. I bought some leopard's claws, the foot of a civet cat and a lion's tail. With these I was able to establish which animal we were talking about.

That did not end the problem, however. The Dowayos 'explained' the relations between these animals with a story: 'A leopard took a lion as wife. They lived in a cave in the mountains and had three children. One day the leopard roared. Two children were afraid and ran away. They became the serval and civet cat. The one who stayed became a leopard. It is finished.'

It seemed natural to ask whether this had happened only once or whether this was the origin of all servals and civet cats. Some said one thing, some another. Some maintained that this was the origin of all civet cats but that servals were born only from servals. Others claimed that servals were born thus but civet cats were the offspring of civet cats alone.

This was no isolated phenomenon. The most straightforward questions about birds, monkeys, or whatever were fraught with the most appalling complexities that seemed to bear precious little resemblance to bland statements about 'The Dowayos believe that . . .' that one reads in standard monographs. What the Dowayos believed was a matter that it was hard to establish by the obvious means of simply asking them. At every stage all sorts of interpretations were involved if one was to be fair to their thought.

So, life continued for a while. My one festival provided fuel for a many a day's research. The fieldworker can never hope to maintain a good rate of work for very long. In my time in Africa, I estimated that I perhaps spent one per cent of my time doing what I had actually gone for. The rest of the time was spent on logistics, being ill, being sociable, arranging things, getting from place to place, and above all, waiting. I had defied the local gods with my intemperate urge to *do* something. I would soon be cut down to size.

8   Rock Bottom

The next period of my stay was without doubt the most unpleasant I have ever spent anywhere, a time when I wallowed in the sin of despair.

The rot set in when I decided to go to Garoua for supplies. The decision was rather thrust upon me; I had nothing left to eat, barely enough petrol to make the city limits and fifteen hundred francs (about £3). Such circumstances are conducive to bold action. I had promised Augustin a lift and we rendezvoused at first light behind the main street in the hope of sneaking out of town without being loaded to the gunwales with millet or gendarmes after a lift. A swift dash freed us from the town and we resigned ourselves to the heaving, wrenching crawl over the worst part of the road, leading down to the tarmac. We never made it. Some five miles short of our goal, I rounded a corner to find that the road had simply disappeared in the rain. It is a bad Western habit to assume that because a road goes into a corner, it will continue round the other side. With a terrifying crunching of metal, we plunged into a foot-deep ditch right across the track.

It was obvious at once that there was something amiss with the steering. It whined and grumbled and doggedly refused to affect the direction of the wheels. Having lived on a Junior Lecturer's salary, I had had precious little to do with cars and was at a loss how best to proceed. Clearly, help was in order. Normally Herbert Brown could be relied upon to mend anything; wondrous tales were told of his mechanical prowess. With two coat hangers and an old plough, he would improvise a gearbox. His engineering solutions were never elegant but often worked. He would return them to customers with the remark, 'It's just a load of junk, but out here nothin' works for long.' Alas, he was away. There was nothing else for it, I still had to get to Garoua. We pushed the vehicle to the side of the road and continued on foot, flagging down a bush-taxi when we reached the tarmac. I did not, at that time, take the inscription on the door 'God's will alone decides' as an omen.

We arrived without further disaster, having carefully obeyed the injunctions painted on the inside of the vehicle telling us not to spit, fight, vomit or break windows. By now, it was nearly midday and Augustin took me to dine in his favourite African restaurant where the choice consisted of take it or leave it. I took it, then left it. I was brought a cow's foot in a large enamel bowl of hot water. When I say 'cow's foot' I do not mean something based upon a cow's foot, but the entire article complete with hoof, hide and hair. Try as I might, there seemed no way of even getting into it. I declared a sudden loss of appetite. Augustin seized it and reduced it to bones with the dedication of a swarm of driver ants.

Two notable successes marked this trip. Firstly, I charmed some money out of the bank to which I had so rashly committed my finances. Secondly, we arranged a lift back to Poli with the *sous-préfet*'s mechanic. This was, I foolishly thought, an incredible stroke of good fortune. After being driven for hours round various Fulani areas of the city on incomprehensible errands, we set off for Poli. The road is very narrow and patronized by huge lorries with trailers hauling cotton and petrol back and forth between Chad and the N'gaoundere rail link. I noted with dismay that when he passed one of these monsters by swerving over to the verge with one wheel inches away from a three-foot drainage channel, the driver closed his eyes tightly.

Nonetheless, we reached my abandoned vehicle as night fell. He made a rapid inspection. There was no problem; all he had to do was hit it. He crawled underneath and there was heard the clang of metal on metal and what I took to be Fulani oaths. Beaming, he emerged. It was not perfect but would get me to Poli whence I could send for a new part.

I was frankly delighted. Augustin and I embarked and set off at a sedate pace. The steering indeed felt a little strange but worked with a certain approximation. The road was covered with owls. They would sit on the surface and fly up to attack the headlights of cars; the slaughter of them on the roads is very great, and they terrify Dowayos. Owls are thought to carry sorcery under their wings at night. Should a man hear the sound of one about his compound or cattle, he immediately seeks remedies against them.

We arrived at the top of the big hill leading down to Poli and began to descend. It was not until we approached a narrow bridge crossing a ravine that I realized that the steering had gone again. I had time to recollect the sharp spikes along either side of the bridge – all that remained of the balustrade after an accident that had killed a *sous-préfet* at this very spot several years before. We struck a tree, bounced off, struck a rock and headed straight for the ravine. I was already standing on the brakes to no great avail. We were poised an instant on the edge and then plunged over.

A sapling caught us neatly and gradually collapsed under the weight. In complete calm, I turned off the engine, asked Augustin if he was all right and evacuated the vehicle. At the top of the ravine, something suddenly snapped in both of us and we sat looking at the jagged rocks and laughed hysterically – not, of course, from amusement, but from some wave of sheer emotion compounded of terror, relief and incredulity. I think we probably sat there quite a while. At this stage, we seemed to have got out of it very lightly. Augustin had bruised his chest. I had hit my head on the wheel and one or two toes, fingers and ribs seemed to have suffered. Hiking into town, we set about a couple of beers Augustin had secreted against dire emergencies. We felt we had qualified.

The next day the full awfulness of the situation was brought home. An inspection of the wreck convinced me that repair would be a protracted and expensive business and that we had indeed been lucky to escape without serious injury. We had a check-up with the local doctor who declared us both unharmed. From the fact that I still have fingers and toes set at odd angles and a lump on two ribs, I infer that his examination failed to show up a number of minor fractures. The worst part was the condition of my jaw. Two teeth at the front seemed very loose and my whole jaw began slowly to swell up, causing me considerable pain.

Hoping for the best, I reverted to Kongle and continued my

researches into leopards and wildcats, dosing myself with Valium to get to sleep at night.

One of my principal concerns now was the classification of disease, and in pursuit of this I spent a lot of time with one traditional healer in particular who had the disadvantage of living at the top of a sheer cliff above Kongle. We would spend hours collecting roots, discussing the identification of disease and the differences between various treatments.

Dowayos, as mentioned, divide diseases between 'infectious diseases', head witchcraft, ancestor interference and pollutions. Only infectious diseases or accidental injuries that may be caused by witchcraft can be helped with herbs. The attribution of one particular disease to a specific cause is quite complex. The names of some diseases refer both to symptoms and a causal agent (like our word 'cold' which implies certain symptoms and a viral cause). Other names are just symptoms (like 'jaundice' that can be the result of many diseases). To tie up symptoms with diseases, various forms of divination are used. A healer may be called to cast the entrails of a chicken into water, the man may be viewed through a glass ball by a specialist who can thus determine his malady. The most common form of divination, however, is to rub the plant *zepto* between the fingers while calling out the various forms of disease that may afflict the man. When the *zepto* breaks, this shows that the correct name has been found. The diviner then moves on to the causative agent – witchcraft, ancestors, etc. Next comes the remedy. Three divinations normally suffice to give full information. If the sick man cannot come to the diviner himself, he should send some of the straw from the roof of his granary, the most private and personal area of a man's compound.

If a named ancestor is held to be responsible, a man is dispatched to the skull house with blood, excrement or beer to fling on the skull of the importuning kinsman.

Pollution diseases usually require the attention of experts - circumciser, sorcerer or rainchief. Often, causes and effects can be linked in a rather oblique fashion. For example, what we would term a sprain is held to hurt because worms have got into the limb; worms come from rain, so only the rainchief can cure them. Contact with the affairs of the dead, on the other hand, involves treatment by the sorcerer and consists of rubbing the garments or other personal belongings of the dead man onto the victim. The worst pollution diseases come from the blacksmith and his wives, the potters. Excessive contact with them, especially with the tools of their trade, causes what one can only term an ingrowing vagina in women and a prolapsed anus in men. The bellows that afflicts men is a remarkably phallic object and the fact that it attacks the anus rather than the penis has to be connected to the 'official' version of circumcision, claiming it to involve sealing of the anus.

Other men set up charms that cause pollution illness to protect their property. A close contact of mine was the clown for the village of Kongle. He was proprietor of the only orange tree in the area and was inordinately attached to me since the time I bought two hundred oranges from him. (I should confess that I had not intended to buy two hundred oranges but twenty; an inadequacy in my handling of numerals lay at the root of the problem.) To protect his tree from the ravages of children, he attached certain plants and goat horns to it so that anyone who stole his oranges would cough like a goat and have to come to him to be cured.

Some Dowayos make a good income from the possession of magic stones that cause everything from toothache to dysentery. Those afflicted have to come to them for the cure. Dowayos see nothing wrong in making money in this way.

Head witchcraft is transmitted from close relatives in peanuts or meat. It fears sharp objects and a boy should therefore not be exposed to it before circumcision or he may bleed to death. At night it wanders around and is said to look like a small chick; this is what is carried under the wings of an owl. It sucks the blood of men and cattle and may kill them. Protection may be had by putting sharp thistles or porcupine quills on the roof of one's hut. After death, skulls are examined for witchcraft. I did not at first grasp that people who die 'of witchcraft' are generally not the victims of witches, but witches whose witchcraft has been injured by such charms: once the witchcraft is injured the owner dies. Dowayos use this to explain the high mortality rate among young men who go to the city to work in the dry season. They are only young – mere boys – who have not learned to control their witchcraft. It is especially excited by the sight of meat on butchers slabs and cuts itself on all the sharp knives lying around there.

It is revealed after death as two spikes under the upper jaw. If these are red or black this means the witchcraft has killed. Where there have been a number of deaths of confirmed witches in a single family, suspicion will normally rapidly centre on a particular relative. In pre-colonial times accused witches were put to the ordeal. They would be required, if male, to drink beer in which the knife of circumcision had been soaked; if guilty, their stomachs would swell up and they would bleed to death. Alternatively, they would be required to drink beer containing the poisonous latex sap of the *dangoh* (*Euphorbica Cameroonica*) cactus. If they did not vomit they would die and be held convicted as charged; if they did vomit, white vomit betokened innocence, red vomit guilt. The guilty would then be hanged by the blacksmith.

On one occasion a woman was universally held to be a witch and to have conveyed the infection to her two daughters, both of whom had died. I was present at the examination of the skull of the second. The head was removed from the corpse by an old man using a bent stick. He was much admired for the dexterity with which he inserted the end in the eye socket and flicked off the head without losing any teeth that drop down into the stomach. The cadaver was some three weeks old and the stench was fairly bad; the man would receive a goatskin from the parents for this service. As usual there was a fair amount of ribald humour. The women were sent away: 'If we bent down to pick up the head and farted you would tell everyone.' They withdrew with considerable peevishness and the men examined the head. In my time in Dowayoland I examined a large number of skulls but could never convince myself that the difference between one held to show witchcraft and one free of it was based upon any perceived morphological distinction. The old men were always unanimous, however. The announcement of the finding of witchcraft was greeted not with anger but quiet satisfaction by the village. The woman was, in fact, a close neighbour of mine and immediately jokes began to fly about to the effect that only a white man, immune like all white men to witchcraft, could live next to her. She seemed annoyed at this slur and offered to walk over the skulls of the dead, in which case, were she the source of their witchcraft, she would die. The husband refused to let her. 'What's the point?' he explained to me. 'She'd only die and then I'd have to buy another wife.'

There was none of the wide-eyed fear I had rather expected in the face of witchcraft; the whole thing was viewed in a rather deadpan, matter-of-fact fashion. Dowayos always stressed to me that there were different sorts of head witchcraft, only one of which was bad. Some forms merely gave a man clean teeth; other forms gave success in farming and involved no other person's disadvantage. They would never quite believe me when I explained that such matters interested me because they did not exist in the land of the white men. I was unaware at that time of the Dowayo pedigree as a reincarnated magician that had been constructed for me. Dowayos would never call me a liar but they had a particular facial expression they would adopt when I was trying to put some particularly blatant falsehood over on them such as the existence of underground trains, or the absence of bridewealth in England.

Healers were, on the whole, only too happy to work with me for the relatively small payment I was able to provide. Their only fear was that I would steal their remedies and set myself up in business. In primitive society knowledge is seldom freely available; rather it belongs to people. A man owns his knowledge. He has paid for it and he would be a fool to give it away without payment to another, just as he wouldn't give away his daughters without brideprice. It was only reasonable that they should charge me. Dowayos justify their remedies by their pedigrees. An old remedy is better than a new one; any innovation is suspect as it does not carry the *imprimatur* of the ancestors. Consequently, there is no attempt to find new remedies.

Healers were initially suspicious of my 'clinic' until they had satisfied themselves that I limited myself to the treatment of infectious diseases with white men's roots and was not in competition with them. One particular case raised certain moral and strategic difficulties. The Chief's brother, who lived several huts away, used to come and visit me quite often. He was a gangling, awkward and affable man who had a reputation for being not too bright. I realized one day that he had not been to see me for several weeks and, on inquiring whether he was away, I was informed that he was dying. He had suffered a severe bout of amoebic dysentery and the healer from up the cliff had been called. The examination of the entrails of a chicken had revealed that he was being afflicted by the spirit of his dead mother who wanted beer. This had been flung upon the skull but there was no improvement. Another healer was called. He revealed that, in fact, the illness derived from another spirit masquerading as the spirit of the man's mother. Offerings were made but the young man still weakened. The Chief's third wife, who had looked after him as a boy, was very distressed and came and wailed outside my hut asking if I had no roots that might save him. It was impossible to refuse, since I indeed had some powerful amoebicides and antibiotics. I explained to everyone that I was not a healer and that I did not know whether my roots might help but that if they wished me to try to heal him I would do so. I had been afraid of alienating the healers by this but they were quite prepared to find that a wrong diagnosis had been made. The man's recovery was swift. He passed from a skeletal condition to good health in a matter of days and there was general rejoicing. The healers were in no way put out. They merely explained that this was a complex case of a man ill with an infectious disease but that various spirits had taken advantage of it to increase his sufferings. They had dealt with the spirits; I had dealt with the disease.

It was only when they were ill that I really felt sorry for Dowayos and felt their way of life to be inferior to our own. Otherwise they enjoyed freedom, held themselves to be wealthy, had clear access to their major forms of sensual gratification in beer and women, and had their self-respect. Once ill, however, they died needlessly in agony and terror. There was no real help for them in the government hospital in Poli. There was a regulation that every patient had to turn up with a half exercise book to keep the records of his case in. Illiterate tribesmen had no need of exercise books and therefore never had one to hand; they were not on sale in Poli and the hospital staff refused to keep them as this was not part of their responsibility according to the rules. Patients would be turned away and refused urgent medical treatment until they could find an exercise book. Inevitably, I became a benefactor in this matter, as did the missions, but the effect was that many Dowayos did not bother to go to the hospital at all. There were doubtless many deaths as the result of this, and I found it impossible to condone the arrogant inhumanity of officials in such circumstances. I was guiltily aware that, when I myself was ill, simply because I was a white man I would be expected to jump queues and receive preferential treatment as did local grandees.

Another sensitive moment cropped up at the visit of a French botanist on a whistle-stop tour through Cameroon researching for a projected botanical atlas showing the distribution of plants in the country. I arrived back in my village one day to find this gentleman ensconced in the schoolhouse while surveying the local flora in six hours flat. The Dowayos, of course, could not see why anyone should be interested in plants for their own sake. It was clear that he was trying to steal Dowayo herbal remedies that he would sell elsewhere at huge profit. He ran to a somewhat larger establishment than I did, having procured his own chickens in preference to the local models and two retainers to attend to his wants. We sat down in the middle of the bush to an absurd dinner, complete with tablecloth and serviettes, while Dowayo children crouched round us in a circle, wide-eyed with curiosity. He kindly explained to me how best to take botanical samples for later identification. Face-to-face with Africa, the differences between a French botanist and an English anthropologist seem minimal and we talked far into the night.

The next day my local healer was more than a little brusque at this outrageous raid staged by my 'brother'. I finally convinced him that we were not even from the same country by referring to the fact that Zuuldibo had offered him beer which he had refused. He was a foreigner, like Herbert Brown at the Protestant mission. The distinction between these races and the English was like that between the terrible Fulani and the good Dowayos.

By our lights, the remedies handed out by traditional practitioners are ineffective or even harmful. So alien to our world view are such practices as rubbing goats' horns on a patient's chest to cure tuberculosis that we do not even bother to check their effectiveness. We can handle them quite well under general principles of sympathetic and contagious magic, so that for the anthropologist they hardly register at all. This aspect of their beliefs never really struck me until I began to work with the rainchiefs; but that must be told in its place.

Most Dowayo remedies are based upon the same three magic plants that are expected to deal with all forms of misfortune from adultery to headache. They divide each into several species that cannot be distinguished by the layman by mere physical inspection. Dowayos would always speak as if they were staunch positivists, never believing anything for which they had no direct sense evidence. 'How do you tell one kind of *zepto*, for example, from another?' I would ask. 'How can I tell whether this is the kind that stops adultery or the kind that heals headaches?' They stared at me in sheer disbelief at such simplicity. 'By trying them,' they would answer. 'How else?' They would then go off into long diatribes about stones that caused rain, people who turned into leopards, bats that vomited their excrement through their nostrils as they had no anus – all in violation of their positivist principles. It was impossible to know in advance how they would react to questioning in this sphere. Sometimes they would rattle out the three different ways of saying 'I do not know' with various degrees of exasperation. On occasions I would actually get a straight answer, but more often it was 'I do not know. I have not seen. How could I know when I have not seen?' I began to earn a reputation as a man who would believe anything.

During this period I at last began to feel I was pulling in some data. I had begun to adapt to the demands of African life and field method. I remembered having read somewhere that gold-mining consisted of shifting three tons of rubbish for each ounce of gold extracted; if this was true, fieldwork had much in common with gold-mining.

My jaw, however, had not healed up; indeed, it had got much worse. An unpleasant mixture of blood and pus had begun to ooze from my gums. The time had come to seek help. I stopped off at the mission and found Herbert Brown, who was delighted to hear of the way in which Africa had confounded all my expectations, justifying as it did his own gloomy view of the Dark Continent. He undertook to attempt a repair of the car, although he could not say quite when it would be completed. If I had known it would take nine months, I would have been less grateful. As it was, I felt at least that I had shifted the burden a bit and hitched a ride on the mail truck to Garoua.

I never understood the reluctance of the mail truck's driver to take Whites in his conveyance; he would take anyone else for a small payment. When it came to a Westerner, he would invoke transport regulations as holy writ and refuse point blank. Sometimes a well-intentioned gendarme would lean on him on my behalf, but the whole process of getting out of Poli without transport added hugely to the frustrations of life. But finally I arrived at Garoua where, I had been informed, there lurked a dentist, the only other one in Cameroon being in the capital. After many red herrings involving putative Red Chinese dentists who turned out to be tractor drivers, I eventually tracked the man down at the local hospital.

Being still at the stage of the Western woolly-minded liberal, I took my place in the queue and waited. After some time, a French businessman arrived. He shouldered his way to the front of the queue and gave the nurse 500 francs. 'Is there a white dentist?' he asked. The nurse demurred 'He's not white but he's from France.' The expatriate considered this and left. I stayed.

As soon as the surgery door opened, I found myself propelled by waiting Africans to the front of the queue. Within was a certain amount of dilapidated dental equipment and a large diploma from the University of Lyons, which reassured me somewhat. I explained the problem to a huge man inside. Without more ado, he seized a pair of pliers and pulled out my two front teeth. The unexpectedness of the attack somewhat dulled my senses to the pain of the extraction. The teeth, he declared, were rotten. Perhaps, he hinted darkly, they had always been rotten. He had removed them. I was cured. I should pay the nurse outside. I sat blankly in the chair, blood gushing down my shirtfront, and tried to make him understand that he could now proceed to the next stage of his treatment. It is not easy to argue in a foreign tongue in the absence of two front teeth; I made little progress. Finally, he understood that I was a difficult patient. Very well, he declared huffily, if I was not content with his treatment, he would bring the dentist himself. He disappeared, leaving me wondering who had just operated upon me. I had fallen into the obvious trap of believing that anyone in a dental surgery, wearing a white coat and prepared to extract teeth, was a dentist.

Another man appeared, also in a white coat. Swiftly, I asked whether he was the dentist. He agreed that he was. This other man was his mechanic; he also repaired watches. A dental repair to bridge the hole in my apparatus would be very expensive. It was very difficult and required great skill. He had that skill. I tried to explain to him that unless I could talk, I could not work. If I could not work, I could not pay him. He brightened visibly. I should return in the afternoon. He would confect a plastic device. As a valued patient, I qualified for an anaesthetic. He injected novocaine into my gums. It seemed a strange thing to do after the operation but I felt too wretched to care.

I spent a somewhat awkward interval wandering around Garoua, gap-toothed and werewolf-fanged. People approaching me crossed the street to avoid passing too close. There was so much blood on my chest that I looked as if I had been mortally wounded. I could only lisp and stutter explanations to inquisitive gendarmes who clearly suspected me of some vile act of human dismemberment.

In the afternoon I returned and received two plastic teeth that balanced precariously on my gums and a bottle of pink liquid to gargle with. I was charged ten times the legal rate for treatment but knew no better than to pay up. As I left, I noticed the syringe I had been injected with lying on the floor.

Learning to cope with this dreadful prosthetic device was a complication I could well have done without. The Dowayos, of course, were delighted with it: many of them have their front teeth filed away to resemble my condition. I asked them why they did this? Was it for beauty? Oh no. Was it – and here the anthropologist was indulging his fancy – to provide for the body an entrance which was the same shape as the gate at the entrance to the village? Oh no, *patron*. They did it, they informed me, so that if a man's jaw locked solid, they could still push food into his mouth and he could eat. Did this happen often? As far as anyone knew it had never happened, but it might. My ability to remove my teeth, and even more, their own ability and willingness to remove themselves in mid-conversation, were matters of great interest to Dowayos.

It was now nearly harvest time and the Dowayos were fitting as many wet-season ceremonies as they could into the last month before the end of the rains. After death there are ceremonies to place a man's bow, which is attached behind the skull-house, and a woman's water-jar, which is returned to her brothers by husband or son. I was particularly keen to see these. Only once all the ceremonies had been witnessed and recorded would any analysis of their rationale or structure become possible.

Matthieu, pleased by the way that my removable teeth had elevated his status, reported that there were rumours that my local healer was about to perform this ceremony for his dead wife. I always hated going up to see him because it involved crawling up a crumbling rock face with precipitous drops, but there was nothing for it. The man had chosen this inhospitable place to live for several reasons. Firstly, it was traditionally the way Dowayos were supposed to live, cultivating the hillsides on terraces so steep that they do so on their knees. Moreover, being several hundred feet higher, the climate was more suited to growing small varieties of millet that were more valued by Dowayos than the gross forms that flourish on the plains. In theory all offerings to the ancestors should be in this higher form of millet and the beer made with it is stronger. Finally, there was less trouble from the ravages of cattle in the fields.

This would be a relatively easy location to work in: mountain villages are cool, the man was sure to make me welcome, and it was not far from my own hut. I checked cameras, recorder, etc., and made a preliminary visit to grease my host's palm and glean his motives for organizing the ceremony and what preparations had been made. This was always a wise move. Once a ceremony was under way, there would be so many marauding kinsmen that no one would have time for an anthropologist's foolish questions. Moreover, it gave me time to look at the sort of answers I was getting and the sort of questions I was putting and see whether they could not be improved on. I would follow this up with a second visit several days after the festival to clear up any points that arose in the heat of performance and check identities, inconsistencies and differences with other villages' ways of conducting the ritual. It was also a chance to get good pictures of ritual paraphernalia that would not have been returned to their owners yet and which might not emerge clearly in photographs taken during the ceremony. I had decided as a matter of policy to send my undeveloped films home and have friends check them there. Having them developed in Cameroon would be both expensive and unreliable, and keeping them for eighteen months in such a climate very risky. It meant that many would be lost in the mail and that I would not be able to see them myself until I returned to England, but on the whole it seemed the wisest course. The great disadvantage was that it considerably increased my contact with the officials at the post office who were past masters at ineptitude and unhelpfulness, even by local standards.

These last few days before the ceremony brought a major change in my conditions of life. I was in town on my mail run when there appeared an unknown truck laden with boxes, barrels and trunks. Unknown vehicles were always grounds for rife speculation. This one contained two unknown white people, a man and a woman. As resident white man it fell to me to go up first and poke my nose into their affairs. We had a conversation in rather awkward French, in the course of which it became apparent that we were all anglophones and my hand, with two broken fingers, was crushed in a manly grip.

Jon and Jeannie Berg, as they revealed themselves, were now missionaries to Poli – colleagues at the Protestant mission of Herbert Brown. They were young Americans, new to Africa, as baffled by the whole experience as I had been. It was Jon's task to look after teaching in the Bible school; Jeannie was his helpmate. We all bore the heavy scent of higher education.

Once they settled in Poli they were the relentless goal of my mail runs. In their agreeable company one could speak English of a sort, eat bread that Jeannie baked in the kitchen, listen to music and talk about things other than millet and cattle. It was Jon's task to communicate to Dowayos 'the meaning of Christianity', as it was mine to establish 'the meaning of Dowayo culture'. We both helped each other to an understanding of the limitations of our mutual endeavours. Jon was the proud owner, moreover, of twelve barrels of trash literature that he generously lent out. I maintain that it was this, above all else, that kept me sane in Dowayoland. Those infinite longueurs between ceremonies, those terrible dull evenings after seven o'clock when all Dowayos were abed, became so much less frustrating with something to read. Fieldwork became the most concentrated literary experience of my life. Never before had I had such an opportunity to read. I read sitting on rocks, half-way up mountains, sitting in streams, crouched in huts by the light of the moon, waiting at crossroads by the light of oil-lamps. I was never without one of Jon's paperbacks. When expectations failed and holy oaths to me were broken, I would simply slip into fieldwork gear, pull out my paperback and outwait the Dowayos.

I acquired an enviable reputation for stubbornness. If someone promised to meet me and did not turn up, I simply sat down with a book and waited until he *did* turn up. I felt that I had finally achieved a Western victory over the Dowayo notion of time.

Jon and Jeannie, apart from solving my transport problem and proving willing to haul supplies from the city, fulfilled several other needs. Jon lent me a key to his office, so I could use it when he was travelling. It had a real desk, the first flat writing surface I had seen in Dowayoland, electric light and paper. These luxuries cannot be appreciated by anyone who has not lived in an African mountain village. I could step through the door and simply leave Dowayoland for several hours at a stretch. I could spread out my notebooks and begin to analyse my data, to detect areas where my knowledge was sketchy, to scent other parts where inquiry might be rewarding, to pursue the demands of abstract thought without interruption or distraction – most un-African pursuits.

All this, of course, lay in the future on our first encounter, but events rather overtook my own expectations. I was engaged, as I mentioned, on the recording of the jar-ceremony. I turned up on the announced day and found, to my surprise, that the ceremony would indeed take place as advertised. I confess that climbing the mountain took rather more out of me than I had expected; by the time I reached the top I could hardly stand, and the world was swimming before my eyes. I recorded the ceremony as best I could, the decoration of the dead woman's jar as a candidate for circumcision, the songs and the dance where a man carried the jar on his head. But something was definitely very wrong. I could hardly keep my eyes open, the weight of my camera seemed unbearable, Dowayo 'explanations' suddenly annoyed me beyond all measure. I was sitting on the wall of the cattle-park, working out the kin-relations between the various participants, when a man warned me not to sit in that particular place on pain of catching a horrible disease. I sought explanations from my assistant. The problem lay, he explained, in certain broken pots over in one corner. Therein accumulated certain gases that might draw the vitamins from my stomach. This gibberish was just too much for me and I found myself in a great rage, rather to my surprise since this was quite typical of the explanations I was used to from Dowayos who could read and write. In my normal frame of mind I would have noted this merely as an attempted translation of a traditional Dowayo perception into a pseudo-Western form. In fact, as I discovered by much painstaking inquiry later, the danger lay in the stones to ensure the fertility of the cattle that were buried under the broken pots. These could interfere with human sexuality and should only be approached by old men well past the age of paternity. In sitting as I was, I was risking my own fertility.

By the end of the ceremony, I was hardly able even to make notes and fled back down the mountain at breakneck speed to collapse on my mud bed. Next day, before the sun rose fully, I crept into town to see the doctor. He looked in my eyes, examined my bright orange urine under the microscope and declared that I had viral hepatitis. 'You haven't had any injections from a dirty needle recently?' he asked. I thought back to the dentist at Garoua. The only cure was a regime of B complex vitamins, plenty of rest and rich diet. Given my current circumstances, this was out of the question. After some two days in bed, I felt rather better and went back up the mountain to finish the inquiry into the jar-ceremony.

Still rather bleary-minded, I continued my work for another week or so until Jon drove out to the village to see me with another missionary from N'gaoundere. I do not recall our conversation. It was something to do with the sexual connotations of penis yams, an example of which I had procured that very day. They exchanged meaningful looks and went into a huddle. It seemed that they were a little concerned at my condition and wanted to give me a lift to the mission hospital at N'gaoundere.

I was far from convinced that such extreme measures were necessary but, luckily for me, they insisted on dropping by the next day on the way out of town. It seemed wise to ponder the matter. Armed with soap, I set out for the swimming-place but, a mere hundred yards from the village, was assailed by a huge bout of fatigue that made it impossible to continue. Sitting down on a convenient rock, I was quite unable to command my legs. It began to rain heavily but motion was still totally beyond me. I recalled that it was my birthday and simply collapsed in tears, in which condition I was discovered by Gaston, a man from a nearby village. I sobbed out my inability to walk and he simply picked me up and carried me back to my hut, where I slept until hauled to the hospital.

9 Ex Africa semper quid nasty

Any African hospital is a shock by Western standards. There is nothing here to remind us of the hushed tones and pastel hues of our institutions. The unpleasant and offensive aspects of the human body are not dealt with in side wards and behind screens; it is very much a public place. When a man is ill, his whole family insist on being there, cooking there, doing the washing, nursing the children and conducting domestic affairs in strident voices as if at home. There are blaring radios, hawkers peddling a hundred forms of trash, long queues of swaddled women and downcast men all clutching pieces of paper like charms. Male nurses cut through them, intent on their own purposes, oblivious to the clutching hands and wailing voices. The environs are an ecological disaster. Every leaf has been plucked to wipe hands, every twig to feed fires, every blade of grass has been pounded to death and the lunar landscape is dotted with neat piles of excrement on which furtive dogs feed.

In the midst of it all is a doctor, usually white, harassed and overworked, rushing from one emergency to another, combining in his own no-frills service the competences of a dozen hospital departments. Here I received treatment in the form of gamma globulin injections that made me incapable of moving my legs for two days and, once more, I was generously taken in from the rain by the Nelsons who clearly decided on a policy of feeding me up.

The great trouble with hepatitis, it seemed, was that it could easily become chronic and dog me to the end of my stay. It was therefore important to identify which of the several varieties I had contracted. This could only be done at Yaounde. Here there was also a proper dentist who could produce a more serviceable dental repair until I got back to England. I was encouraged to seek this by the obvious distress of Westerners when my teeth flew out spontaneously in the midst of eating, talking or other forms of ordinary activity.

Financial disaster loomed on all fronts. Money was still not getting through to me. The bank was incapable of following the simplest instructions and my indebtedness to the mission was becoming something of an embarrassment. Now I had to face further expenditure on vehicle and personal repairs. In desperation I sent a telegram to my college asking them to advance me £500 to get me out of difficulties. If they could cable it to me, I would pick it up at the British Embassy in Yaounde.

My physical collapse had come at a relatively convenient time. The main ritual season was over and the harvest, which I particularly wanted to witness, had not yet begun. I had about three weeks to refit and return to the field. With luck I might just make it. Gritting my dentures, I set off for Yaounde.

Being in a delicate condition, I opted for taking a couchette and damn the expense. This was surprisingly clean and comfortable and in a style that seemed to hail from the Tierra del Fuego Railroad Co. of about 1910. My chances of a good night, however, were destroyed by the efforts of the attendant to install me in a compartment together with a formidable Lebanese woman and her willowy daughter. The attendant pointed me to a bunk and I stowed my kit and settled down to sleep. Abruptly he was seized by this Levantine virago. 'No man sleeps in the same room as my daughter till she is married,' she hissed. 'She is a virgin,' she elaborated. We both regarded her with renewed interest. I attempted to disclaim all ambitions upon the physical charms of her offspring. The girl giggled. The attendant ranted. I was ignored.

The attendant treated us to a long reading from the regulations despite constant heckling from the woman. This dispute went round and round with that lack of purpose that characterizes African arguments.

'I know a director of the railway. I shall have you fired.'

'My brother is an Inspector of Immigration. I will have you deported.'

'Savage!'

'Whore!'

117

An undignified tussle took place in the doorway, ending in great quantities of spitting. The girl and I exchanged looks of mute sympathy. It was time to be dogmatic and I roused myself with difficulty. The woman seemed to fear an attempt to assault her daughter from the rear and leaped to interpose herself with clenched fists. Profiting from her distraction, the attendant seized her from behind and began dragging her howling into the corridor. A large crowd, consisting largely of travelling policemen, gathered to watch with serene detachment, while meaner spirits urged the combatants on.

As for me, I limped off down the corridor where I found almost all the couchettes empty and chose one at random. The attendant regarded this as a vile defection and favoured me with his views on the Lebanese at great length until I bribed him to simply go away. At intervals throughout the night I would hear the door of the compartment down the corridor open as the lady sentinel spotted her enemy passing and hurled abuse after him. The next morning as we pulled into Yaounde, he was dedicating himself to preventing her getting a porter, while she attempted to pour her drinking water over him.

I rendezvoused with French friends, whom I'd met when I'd first arrived, at the usual bar and we gossiped about what had happened to whom. Most of the absentees seemed to have fallen foul of the extremely virulent venereal diseases that haunt West Africa, social life being so dull that fornication is the chief distraction. The souvenir vendors, to my horror, recognized me as the one who had passed through without buying anything the first time and were determined not to let me escape again.

Whereas when I first arrived in Cameroon I had been greatly impressed by the ugliness and squalor of Yaounde, I now saw the city as a haven of beauty and good taste, brimming over with the comforts of civilization. Something drastic seemed to have happened to my standards in the few intervening months. I found myself also unmoved by rather shocking collocations of wealth and poverty As we sat at the café, in mainly white company, a small child stood on the pavement and, driven by I know not what path to political radicalism at so tender an age, began to rail against foreigners. The clientele of the café found this hugely

118

amusing and threw coins that the child scrabbled in the dirt to pick up.

I was soon installed in my friends' flat and noted once again how different are the priorities of French and English young people. The unattached English or Americans one meets in such circumstances live either off the land or out of tins, but the French insist on their *cuisine*. Their lives, when not teaching, consisted of motor rallies in the jungle, parties in the Embassy area and touristic enterprises. One was an enthusiastic taxidermist and specialized in the stuffing of pangolins (scaly ant-eaters). These, it seems, are extraordinarily difficult beasts to kill and he was always experimenting in new ways of doing them to death. It was not unusual to find the bath full of remarkably lively pangolins that he had purportedly just drowned, or the lid being forced off the freezer by pangolins he had 'frozen to death'.

By a strange coincidence, the new doctor at the Polyclinique turned out to be known to me, being the boyfriend of the sister of an old friend, and we had once met in a bar in La Rochelle. It was extremely comforting to find the world such a small place and working on such very African principles of extended kinship. He arranged for me to have blood tests, a process that I regarded with somewhat mixed feelings. It seemed counterproductive to have needles stuck in me as the cure for having needles stuck in me.

The next day I called in at the Embassy to see if there was any trace of my money. To my surprise, I discovered that I was the subject of much diplomatic activity. Hugely exaggerated reports of my maiming and disfigurement had reached them via the Foreign Office in London, and a member of the Embassy was even toying with the idea of going beyond the confines of the capital to look for me. Characteristically they went into elaborate explanations of the many ways in which they couldn't help me. They did arrange for me to jump the queue to see the dentist, but denied firmly all knowledge of money.

I was forced to spend two weeks in Yaounde while my teeth were being repaired and took full advantage of it to eat meat, bread and, on one exquisite day, a cream cake. (When I returned to England I adopted a policy of eating two a day until I regained normal weight.) There is no more cheering experience than being able to walk about again after an illness. Life was full of hedonistic pleasures. I went to dinner with a man who ran the local tobacco company and could not explain my sudden, all-enveloping sense of well-being until I realized that I was sitting in an upholstered armchair for the first time in four months. In Dowayoland, I sat on rocks or on the Chief's rickety deckchairs, at the mission on stiff-backed chairs. There were cinemas too, with various luxurious features, such as systems whereby you could hear the soundtrack at the back without having to rely on word of mouth passed from the front of the house. Best of all, they had roofs not made of corrugated iron so that a heavy shower did not obliterate everything.

But this euphoria was short-lived. Life for the Whites centred on the various bars where they forgathered in the evening to share each others' boredom and complain about Yaounde. Since I was absolutely forbidden alcohol on pain of a relapse, these places were infinitely boring for me, and in the end I was not sorry to return up-country; other considerations apart, I was convinced that the Dowayos would have begun the harvest the moment my back was turned.

I dropped in at the hospital to pick up the results of my blood tests. The first report informed me I was suffering from 'sample lost'. The second diagnosed 'no reagent for this test'. Predictably, it had been a waste of time. However, I felt much improved physically and could pronounce most of the basic sounds of the English language with my new teeth. Only my finances had suffered. It was not for several more months that the Embassy discovered that money *had* in fact been sent to me and was lying in a drawer somewhere. I was impressed by their tact in sending me an invitation to the Queen's birthday party so that it arrived the week *after* the event; on the back someone had written, 'The ambassador will not be surprised if you are unable to come.'

I regained N'gaoundere without incident, rendezvousing with Jon and Jeannie for a lift back to Poli. Reinforcements had just arrived from the States in the form of the Blue family whose patriarch, Walter, was to teach at the mission school. He, Jon and I rapidly became soul-mates. Walter, soon established as Vulch thanks to the locals' rendering of his name as 'vulture', was a *Times* crossword addict and spent tortured hours wrestling with them on the veranda, groaning and whooping in alternating despair and exultation. He was also highly musical and soon acquired exclusive rights to a wizened and wheezy piano that had suffered much from damp and termites; it was only much later when he gained access to a more finely tuned instrument that I realized that he could play. His wife Jacqui was the perfect foil, firmly in charge of practical matters: making clothes, keeping hens, hitting pieces of wood with hammers, producing children that Vulch would dandle absently while solving a crossword. Through the house passed a constant stream of visitors; they always seemed glad of more. Arriving from the bush, one never knew quite who would be in residence, luggage laid out among the seething children, cats, dogs and chameleons that variously constituted the ménage.

I was beginning to feel rather less alone in Cameroon. It seemed that the worst had happened and been somehow overcome. I had found friends not too distant from my field location. I had a bolt-hole for when disease, depression and isolation struck me down. I could now get ahead with the work I had come here for.

10 Rites and Wrongs

I had been away just over three weeks but was encouraged to note that the millet by the roadside was not yet ready for harvesting.

Since reading Malinowski's fanatical tirades against anthropology from the mission veranda, such spots have assumed great attractions for me and I always found them pleasant and profitable places from which to contemplate Africa. The main road to town passed just in front, behind lay the mountains lit up by the moon. It was a splendid place for being both nosey and idle.

As I sat enjoying the view and benign warmth after the coolness of N'gaoundere, wafts of drumming blew in from the mountains. Once again, I felt rather like the archetypal white man in one of those sternly wholesome films the British made in the '40s, listening to the natives far out in the hills and wondering whether this signified the massacre we had all feared. In fact I could recognize the sound of the deep death-drum. Someone was being buried, a rich man. With the echoes from the mountains, it was difficult to tell where the sound was coming from. I asked the cook, Ruben, whether he knew. He told me the sound came from Mango; in fact it came from my own village which was where I had placed it. My sense of duty beckoned me forth; hitherto I had not witnessed a major male burial. I bade my friends farewell and headed out to Kongle by the light of a borrowed torch.

As I walked into the village I met my assistant who welcomed me warmly and asked for an advance on his wages. The death was indeed that of a rich man in the most distant part of Kongle, a compound where I had good contacts through a man named Mayo. Mayo was an old friend of Zuuldibo's father and was treated by the administration as chief of Kongle in defiance of the wishes of the people and the rules of inheritance. Zuuldibo's father had hit on the notion that if the administration could levy taxation, then so could he. He had raised a special tax for himself and been most aggrieved when told that this was not permitted. There had developed a great feud between the *sous-préfet* and the people of Kongle, and Mayo, who had always had the more tedious aspects of chiefship foisted on to him, was regarded as the agent of the government. Strangely, Mayo and Zuuldibo remained the best of friends and Mayo was a universally popular figure. I thought him quite the nicest Dowayo I ever met. He was generous, helpful, high-spirited and had put himself out to assist me on numerous occasions. I was pleased to note that Matthieu had just returned from Mayo's village and had made notes on the proceedings.

We set out at dawn the next morning for the 'place of death'. Mayo insisted on bringing out a deckchair, covered, I noted, with burial cloth, and setting it up right beside the body where it considerably impeded the activities of the participants.

The body had already been wrapped once with the skin of a steer slaughtered for this purpose by his brothers. Round and round the village ran women in leaves of mourning, banging empty calabashes together and wailing. To one side of the special enclosure for male dead sat the widows, staring stonily ahead of them. Foolishly, I sought to greet them; they are not allowed to speak or move. The men considered this a great joke and giggled and sniggered as they wrapped the cadaver. Other kinsmen, especially affines, were bringing in material to wrap the body, skins, cloth and bandages. The dead man's son-in-law arrived, bringing his wife. He has to stand her in the cattle-park and fling his offerings at her belly, indicating the link between himself and the family of the dead. Wife-givers to the family of the dead fling their offerings in the faces of his kinsmen. This is normally a gesture of insult and accurately indicates the relations of respect and inferiority a man shows towards his wife's parents and their superiority with regard to him.

There was a great deal of joking going on between the men. Later, I was to learn that these were men circumcised at the same time as the deceased. They have a lifelong obligation to insult each other jokingly and make free with each others' property.

Suddenly there was a torrential downpour and everyone melted away. 'Where have they gone?'

'They have gone off to defecate in the bush.'

At the time, I naïvely assumed that this was merely an interval in the ceremony where those who had been occupied here since early morning would break off by common consent and relieve themselves in the bush before continuing. Only later would I find that it was an integral part of the ceremony – an oblique reference to the reality of circumcision between brothers, an admission that the anus is not sealed. Matthieu, Mayo and I retired to a hut until the rain blew over and Mayo told me of what the men do at the crossroads in the early morning after a death. It was typical of Mayo that he would volunteer information of this kind whereas it had to be dragged out of most men.

The men go out to the crossroads. The clowns and sorcerers are there too. The brothers of circumcision are there. Two face each other, sitting down. They put grass over their heads. One says, 'Give me your cunt.' The other replies, 'You may have my cunt.' One copulates with the other. They do it with a stick. A man sets fire to the grass. They shout. They join the other men. It is finished.

Mayo found this whole episode quite hilarious and literally fell about laughing. It was only polite to do likewise but my mind was elsewhere trying to 'make sense' of this information. Dowayo festivals always made me feel punch-drunk, overwhelmed by the suggestiveness yet lack of definition of their symbolism. I felt the whole time that there was a large chunk missing, some major and obvious fact that no one had bothered to tell me so that I was simply holding the whole thing upside down and looking at it all wrong. I already suspected what it was – circumcision – but no one was quite ready to talk about that yet. I would have to piece it together very slowly over the next months. In fact, this whole episode is simply an abbreviated version of what happens when a boy is circumcised, and derives its structure from that, as do all festivals in Dowayoland. All life crises, all major calendrical festivals are depicted in terms of circumcision. This is why circumcision dress keeps cropping up in the most unlikely places, the dead woman's water-jar, the wrapping given a corpse.

There was a shout outside. While we had been inside, the men had returned and tied a red hat to the body, just like the circumcision candidate wears. The corpse was jostled and threatened with circumcision. Sometimes a naked boy is required to lean back against the body and a red thread is cut away from his penis simulating circumcision.

Matthieu and I stayed far into the night recording songs and collecting gossip of all kinds; the tapes would provide employment for some time to come.

We had hardly returned to the village and set about our first meal of the day when we heard that there was to be another skull-festival nearby, perhaps tomorrow, perhaps the next day. Nothing would happen at the burial for perhaps two days while the body was 'lying in state', so that could be left simmering while we went over to the other big event.

While we were eating Matthieu had assumed a sly expression that I had come to know and fear. He was always so long working round to something that it was a blessed relief when he came to the point. At last he came out with it. While I was away he had spent his time visiting relatives but also in sorting out the contents of my hut. He had come across an old suit dumped in the bottom of a suitcase. This I had brought with me on the advice of a colleague: 'You'll need at least one suit.' I never discovered why. I had carried the thing around with me for months awaiting an occasion to put it on, and had finally relegated my colleague's tip to a long list of 'crazy and useless advice for fieldworkers'. Matthieu, however, had other ideas. He requested earnestly that I wear the suit to the skull festival. It would impress people, he claimed. I refused point-blank. He sulked. Well then, there was another matter. I should have a cook. It was not right that I cook myself; moreover, on occasions such as today it would have been a fine thing to return and find food awaiting. He had a 'brother'; he would bring him. For the sake of peace and quiet I agreed to talk to him, but had secretly not the slightest intention of saddling myself with a domestic establishment.

Next day I was roused by Matthieu even before dawn. He was all smiles. He had a surprise for me. The cook he had mentioned, his brother, he had sought him out. He had made breakfast. This consisted of intestines burnt black in copious quantities of cooking oil. I hated the way Dowayos swamped everything in oil. The cook was presented to me to receive my congratulations. He was a youth of about fifteen who had the peculiarity of having six fingers on both hands. This quite distracted and interested me. I would have to find out about notions concerning cripples and deformity. The youth attributed his success at cooking to the contact he had had with Whites in Garoua. Had he perhaps been a cook there? No, a dustman. I felt tired; this was a problem I would have to come back to when I was feeling stronger. I would talk to him again this evening.

In keeping with Dowayo notions of time, the festival was not at the stage it should have been; this had the advantage of enabling me to see parts the Dowayos had kept quiet about. This, in all fairness, was not their fault. I had asked to see the 'throwing on the skulls', my understanding being that this was the name for the whole ceremony. It was the name but also, unfortunately, the technical term for just that part where excrement and blood were thrown on the skulls. Thus when I asked to see 'throwing on the skulls' that was precisely what I had got. Meanwhile all sorts of provocative acts were being performed by other people I did not know were involved at all. The men, for example, performed a narcissistic dance with mirrors. Brothers of circumcision were required to climb on the roofs of the huts of the dead and rub their anuses against the roof ridge. Women performed all sorts of strange acts with penis yams that quite baffled me until I discovered that they were a mere adaptation of what boys do after they have been circumcised. In other words, the widows of the dead are treated as if they have just been circumcised after taking their final leave of their dead husbands. The common feature is that they are now totally reincorporated into normal life after a period of exclusion from it. Their husbands, who undergo the skull-ceremony, are treated as if they have just been circumcised. The common feature here is that they may now be placed in the skull-house where the circumcision ritual itself has its final climax.

Very little of this was clear to me at the time, of course. I was far too busy just writing it down to be able to even speculate what it was that I was noting with such industry. I often simply fired questions at random in the hope of hitting something to ask further questions about. The problem of working in the area of symbolism lies in the difficulty of defining what is data for symbolic interpretation. One is seeking to describe what sort of a world the Dowayos live in, how they structure it and interpret it. Since most of the data will be unconscious, this cannot simply be approached by asking about it. A Dowayo, when faced with the question, 'What sort of a world do you live in?' is rather less able to answer than we ourselves would be. The question is simply too vague. One has to piece it all together bit by bit. Possibly a linguistic usage will be significant, a belief or the structure of a ritual. One then seeks to incorporate it all into some sort of scheme.

For example, I have already explained that blacksmiths are set apart from the rest of Dowayos and that this separateness finds its expression in rules enforcing separate cultivation, eating, sex, drawing of water. An anthropologist would suspect that other forms of communication would also stress the separateness of blacksmiths; there might well be beliefs about language, for instance. I found that blacksmiths were supposed to speak with a particular accent, different from other Dowayos; their sexual isolation might be stressed by beliefs about incest or homosexuality. The last I found a particularly awkward area. My opportunity to broach the subject came on the occasion of the castration of a bull whose testes were being eaten by parasitic worms. I was interested to note that, had several cattle been due for castration, this would have been performed in the circumcision grove where boys are cut, another example of the identification of cattle and men. As all the cattle were driven in so that the diseased one could be caught, two yearlings tried to mount each other. I pointed this out, hoping that similar practices would be imputed to some group, with luck, blacksmiths. The further I went in my questioning, the more awkward and embarrassing it became. The truth seems to be that homosexual practices are largely unknown in West Africa except where white men have spread the word. Dowayos were incredulous that such things were possible. Such behaviour in animals was always interpreted as 'They are fighting over women'. Males will have much more physical contact than is normal in our own culture but it carrie no sexual overtones: friends walk hand in hand; often young me will sleep entwined together but this is not thought to involv sexuality. Dowayos who had not seen me for some time woul often sit in my lap and stroke my hair, amused at my emba rassment at such public behaviour. So my hopes that smith might have a reputation for homosexuality were unfounded – bu they did eat dogs and monkeys; most Dowayos will refuse bot An anthropologist would explain that this is because both a too close to humans. Eating them, therefore, is the culinar equivalence of incest or homosexuality.

And so one picks one's way through the morass of data by process of constant error and revision. On this particular day however, I confess to being more preoccupied with the proble of my cook and how to disembarrass myself of his dubiou services. Fortunately an excellent solution finally occurred to m I would employ him as one of the people to build my projecte new house. Feelings would be spared all round. He wou doubtless be better at throwing mud than cooking food.

Besides the other interests of this festival, it provided me wit another opportunity to speak to the Old Man of Kpan, since th event was happening in his own back garden. As usual, he wa surrounded by a considerable retinue, someone holding a re umbrella over his head, and sated with beer. He was eager t compare dentures and, finding his own to be a vastly more sophist cated device, was moved to invite me to visit him in a month time. He would send me word.

The rainy season was now officially over and it would not rai again for five or six months, a matter of great comfort to m since I have always hated rain. On the way back from the skull however, there was a remarkable storm. It began with a fair moaning sound in the mountains that grew to a dull roa Looking up at the sky, we could see huge clouds building an swirling round the peaks. It was obvious we should not reach th village before its full force hit us. The wind raced across the plai tearing at the grass and ripping leaves from the trees. It was clea to Matthieu that this was no ordinary storm but a person demonstration by the rainchief of his power. I must confess tha had I not been a totally prejudiced Westerner I should have been inclined to agree with him, for the storm was quite remarkable. The rain lashed us so that we were saturated from head to foot in seconds and shivering from the cold. The buffeting of the wind was so violent that it tore the buttons off our shirts and we were obliged to call a halt at a log bridge. This consisted of a split tree trunk covered with moss that spanned a gorge some forty feet deep. It was simply impossible to teeter across this in the wind and so we sat down to wait, Matthieu terrified that the Old Man would send lightning to kill us. I told him that white men cannot be struck by lightning so he should stick to me and no harm could come of it. He believed this at once. West Africa has apparently the highest incidence in the world of people being struck by lightning. I remember sitting there thinking that, since almost every vehicle has a *motorjo*, a man whose task it is to tie down baggage and climb on the roof to let goods down for passengers, the expression 'my postilion has been struck by lightning' is probably more useful here than anywhere else on Earth.

Finally, the fury died down and we regained the village. The story of the storm rapidly did the rounds and I spent the evening chatting quite openly about rainchiefs; overnight it had become an acceptable subject of conversation.

Some of the Dowayos had already begun to harvest, although it was rather early, and it was clearly time for me to become ubiquitous in the fields. For the harvest a threshing floor must be constructed. This consists of a shallow depression scooped in the earth and plastered with mud, cattle excrement and sticky plants to form a firm base. It must be protected against witchcraft with spiky remedies: thistles, barbs of millet stems or bamboo, even porcupine quills are used. Here the heads of the cut millet are normally allowed to dry for several days before being beaten with sticks to dislodge the grain. This is very hard work and hated by Dowayos. The husk is fiercely irritating to the skin and even the toughened hides of Dowayos come up in huge weals. They sit around alternately beating and drinking, scratching with an unrestrained enjoyment that brooks no modesty. I became especially interested in the threshing floor. Everywhere such places are the focus of symbolic elaboration and there is a complex of prohibitions attaching to them in Dowayoland. I already knew that there was a special class of 'true cultivators' who had to take special precautions. I had already arranged to visit one of these for his harvest in some two weeks time and would find out then about his special place in the cultural system. I had made a point of getting on good terms with the local women, knowing that they would be a good source on such matters, being prone to having their sexuality disrupted by breaches of taboos, and had learned that a pregnant woman should never go inside a threshing floor. This was not what I had expected. Elsewhere in Dowayoland human sexuality and plant fertility are held to affect each other beneficially. For example the first time that a girl menstruates she is shut up for three days in the grinding hut where millet is made into flour. Only those linked by marriage can accept germinated millet. Blacksmiths, with whom sexual relations are forbidden, should not enter a woman's field if millet is growing there. In other words, a series of parallels is established by the culture between various stages of the millet cycle and the sexual processes of women. In accordance with this, I would have expected childbirth and threshing to be paired off as well. It would have fitted my model very well if a cure for difficult childbirth had been to sit the woman in the threshing circle. I puzzled about this for a long time. I even borrowed Jon's office for a day while he was away to sit down with my notes and try to find out what was wrong. If this was incorrect, I might well have to scrap everything I had worked out thus far concerning the 'cultural map' of the Dowayos.

I decided to have a word with my favourite female informant, Mariyo, the Chief's third wife. We had become good friends after my drugs had cured the Chief's younger brother; I was interested in her for several reasons. She lived just behind my own hut and I could not help but notice the incessant streams of farts, coughs and deafening eructations that issued from that area after dark. I felt great sympathy for her as one whose guts were as little suited to Dowayoland as my own. One day I mentioned this to Matthieu who gave out a loud scream of laughter and ran off to share my latest folly with Mariyo. About a minute later, a loud scream of laughter came from her hut, and thereafter I could chart the progress of the story round the village as hysteria hit one hut after another. Finally Matthieu returned, weeping and weakened by laughter. He led me to Mariyo's compound and pointed to a small hut directly behind my own. Inside lived the goats. Being unversed in the lore of goats, I had been unaware of their human-sound detonations. After this, Mariyo and I were stuck with a joking relationship where we could only communicate by pulling each others' legs. Dowayos have many such relations, both with specific classes of kinsmen and with sympathetic individuals. At times they are enormously diverting, at others vastly tedious, since they take no account of mood.

As the result of our joking sessions, Mariyo was a very relaxed informant and accepted my stern separation of joking from 'asking about things'. She was the only Dowayo I ever met who seemed to have some inkling of what I was after. On one occasion I asked her about the special star-shaped haircuts that female kin wear at a dead woman's jar ceremony. Did they wear them on any other occasion? She answered in the negative, as any Dowayo would but, unlike the others, added, 'Sometimes the men do,' and went on to give me a list of occasions when men cut their hair in this fashion. Since most female rites can only be understood as derived from male rites, this gave me the clue to their interpretation and opened up a whole new line of inquiry that paired designs on the human body with decorations on pots and native ideas of conception that allow the woman to be viewed as a more or less flawed vessel.

I had gleaned the information regarding pregnant women and threshing floors from other female informants, so I was curious what Mariyo would tell me. I worked round to it gradually. How was a threshing floor made? What happened there? Was there anything one most not do on a threshing floor? Was there anyone who must not enter there? Once again, she replied that pregnant women must not enter, 'At least,' she added, 'not until the child is fully formed and ready to be born.' This put the matter in quite a different light. She went on to explain that if a pregnant woman appeared on the threshing floor she would give birth too soon. So my pairing of stages of millet and female fertility was saved. It is impossible to explain to a layman the deep satisfaction that comes from such a simple piece of information as this. It serves as a vindication of years of teaching of platitudes, months of disease, loneliness and boredom, hours of asking foolish questions. In anthropology, moments of validation are few and this one came as a needed morale restorative.

But, as usual in Africa, doing a methodical job could not long be allowed to disrupt a dozen minor concerns and I was forced to take a day off to wage war on the various forms of animal life that had invaded my hut. Lizards I could live with. They ran about in the roof, darting from beam to beam. Their only inconvenience was their habit of defecating on one's head. Goats were a constant curse one had learned to take precautions against. I had a standing feud with one old billy-goat who loved nothing better than to creep into my compound at two o'clock in the morning and jump up and down on my cooking pots. Chasing him away secured relief only for an hour or so; after that he would come sneaking back and perform an encore, kicking my gas cylinder with his back hooves. The worst thing about him was his stench. Dowayo goats stink so badly that it is possible, when trekking in the bush, to tell whether a male goat has been along the same track in the last ten minutes by smell alone. I finally defeated him by subborning the affections of the Chief's dog, Burse, who was hopelessly addicted to chocolate. Giving him one square every evening ensured that he spent the night outside my hut and chased all goats away. Thereafter he introduced his wife and children into the family business and proved a considerable drain on supplies. Dowayos were vastly amused to see my retinue of dogs who would follow me for miles in the bush and sometimes nicknamed me 'the great hunter'.

Termites were a constant threat to all paper. They had a cunning habit of invading books from the inside and devouring them so that externally they appeared perfect while consisting of the merest wafer-thin shell. A short bout of chemical warfare routed them.

Mice were more infuriating. They stonily ignored my food. Like all other life-forms in Dowayoland they were addicted to millet; the only thing I had that they liked was plastic. They devoured the hose for the water-filter in a single night. They made concerted attacks on my camera. What I hated worst about them was their clumsiness as they crashed and thudded from one piece of equipment to another. Their fate was sealed one appalling night when I woke up in the darkness to feel a quivering form on my chest. I lay there immobile, convinced it was a deadly green mamba curled up directly over my heart. I tried to estimate its dimensions. Should I lie there and hope it would go away? Alas, I am a very untidy sleeper and feared that I might well fall asleep and turn over onto it with fatal consequences. I decided that my best move was to count to three and leap up, throwing it off. I counted, uttered a loud yell and flung myself sideways, leaving a goodly part of my knee on the raised edge of the bed. With an unerring dexterity that quite impressed me at the time, I snatched up my torch and shone it on my attacker. There, transfixed in the beam, trembled the smallest mouse I have ever seen. I felt quite ashamed until, in the morning, I discovered it had tried to eat my dentures. That hardened my heart and I made a tour of the village collecting mouse-traps. In a single night I killed ten mice which the children ate.

Far worse than these, however, were cicadas. Ten million cicadas scattered around the hills of Dowayoland produce that pleasant hum that is the hallmark of evening in tropic climes. A single cicada trapped in your hut is a recipe for insanity. They have a curious ability to secrete themselves into small crevices. It is strangely difficult to get a directional fix on their sound. In light they are completely silent. In darkness, they produce the most piercingly strident rasping screech. The only way to detect them was to saturate the area with the contents of a can of insecticide that optimistically displayed images of choking cockroaches, gasping flies, mosquitoes going into tailspins, etc. This was just enough to make them break cover and career woozily over the floor where they could be dispatched with about ten blows from a heavy object. After several sleepless nights the violence and rage required for such a proceeding comes quite naturally.

What had really provoked me to a declaration of all-out war was the discovery that scorpions were nesting in one corner of the hut where I kept my spare pair of shoes. Having picked these up in all innocence, I was appalled when a large, snapping scorpion rushed out and made straight for me. Shrieking in most unmanly fashion, I retreated through the door where stood a Dowayo waif of about six who looked at me quizzically. Stress had somewhat disrupted my lexicon and I could not find the word for 'scorpion'. 'There are hot beasts within!' I cried in an Old Testament voice. The child peered inside and with an expression of profound disdain stamped the scorpions to death with his bare feet. (For the benefit of others, let me point out that scorpions are rarely fatal but their sting can cause severe pain. It is treated by immersing the area in cold water and taking antihistamine tablets that are issued as standard for hay fever.)

Dowayos were always surprised that I found snakes and scorpions as horrifying as I did but had actually been known to avoid running down that most horrible of birds, the owl. On one occasion I had been seen to pick up a chameleon, whose bite is held to be deadly, after some children had been tormenting it, and place it on a tree. This was an act of great folly. My most useful madness was that I was prepared to handle the claws of the ant-eater. Dowayos would not touch these since if they did so their penises would permanently acquire their drooping shape. The claws could be used to kill a man by embedding them in the fruit of the baobab tree and calling out the name of the intended victim; when the fruit drops, he will die. Dowayos who had killed an ant-eater would publicly summon me and present me with the claws as an earnest of their peaceful intentions to fellow villagers. I would then have to carry them up into the hills and bury them away from frequented places. My role as a cosmological pollution control officer was much appreciated.

I gathered from travellers that the millet of my 'true cultivator' was not yet ready for harvesting, so I was able to settle back and watch the latest distraction – an election in Kongle. The *sous-préfet* had summoned all the villagers at a certain place and time so that he could talk to them about it and the outstanding problem of the chiefship. In fact he never turned up, leaving them all sitting under a tree for two days before they drifted back to the fields. Several days later there appeared a *goumier* in the village. These unpleasant people are ex-soldiers used by the central government to ensure obedience in recalcitrant villages where gendarmes cannot keep an eye on things. They take up residence for long periods, living off their hosts, and bully them into doing whatever is demanded of them. In areas where people are ignorant of their rights, or know perhaps how little store to set by them, they exert a considerable tyranny. This particular individual was to ensure that polling booths were prepared for the elections. Hitherto Dowayos had shown themselves very unimpressed by national politics; their enthusiasm was to be stimulated.

All Dowayos, male and female, were to report on the appointed day and vote. It is the Chief's responsibility to ensure a good turn-out and Mayo humbly accepted this as his lot while Zuuldibo sat in the shade calling out instructions to those doing the work. I sat with him and we had a long discussion on the finer points of adultery. 'Take Mariyo,' he said. 'People always tried to say she was sleeping with my younger brother, but you saw how upset she was when he was ill. That showed there was nothing between them.' For Dowayos sex and affection were so separate that one disproved the other. I nodded wisely in agreement; there was no point in trying to explain that there was another way of looking at it.

At the polling booths democracy was in full swing. One man was being upbraided for not bringing all his wives. 'They would not come.' 'You should have beaten them.' I asked several Dowayos what issue they were voting for. They stared at me blankly. You took your identity card, they explained, and gave it to the official over there who stamped it and your vote was marked. Yes, but what were they voting for? More blank stares They had already explained, you took your card . . . Not one of them knew what the election was for. No negative votes were accepted. At the end of the day's proceedings it was felt that not enough votes had been recorded, so everyone was made to vote again. I happened to be in a cinema the week the results were announced with something over ninety-nine per cent of voters choosing the single candidate put up by the only party I took it as a healthy sign that the audience, safely anonymous in the darkness, hooted with derision.

But in the village everyone took the voting very seriously

indeed, in accordance with regulations. Identity cards were meticulously checked, care was taken to place the stamps exactly in the space provided on the card, the percentage of villagers voting was calculated with precision, the registers were transferred from one official to another with much signing of receipts. No one seemed to see any contradiction between such painstaking observation of minutiae and the blatant disregard of the principles of democracy.

It was the same at the schools. They are all weighed down with an incredible bureaucratic apparatus for strictly determining which pupils shall be expelled, which promoted and which obliged to take a year again. The amount of time spent in the abstruse calculation of 'averages' with arcane formulae is at least equal to that spent in the classroom. And at the end of this, the headmaster arbitrarily decides that the marks look too low and adds twenty across the board, or he accepts bribes from a parent and simply changes marks, or the government decides that it has no need of so many students and invalidates its own examinations. At times it becomes bad farce. It is impossible not to smile at the sight of question papers being guarded by gendarmes with sub-machine guns when the envelope they are in has been opened by a man who sold the contents to the highest bidder several days before.

After this interlude it was time to go off to my 'true cultivator' for the harvest. This involved a trek of some twenty miles and the temperatures were climbing daily. It was a matter of some importance to decide whether to walk the distance at night when it was cooler, or hope for a lift if one set out in full daylight. In the end I opted for the latter course and was lucky enough to run into one of the French Catholic priests commuting between two mission stations. He kindly embarked us and we had a most agreeable trip as he told me his theory of Dowayo culture. It homed in on sexual repression. Everything was 'about' sex. The wooden forks set up when a man is killed are, on one side a penis, on the other a vagina; the stress on circumcision represents a deeper uncertainty about castration; the lies about circumcision involving sealing of the rectum are a sure sign that the Dowayos, as a race, are anally obsessed. But he had not only read his manuals of psychology; he had also read anthropology. On examination, this remark meant that he had read a little on the Dogon, a most articulate and self-analytical tribe of Mali. He shook his head sadly over the Dowayos. After all the years he had spent among them they had still not told him their myths or about the primal egg. Having learned that the Dogon were not exactly like the French, he could not cope with the idea that the Dowayos were not exactly like the Dogon.

It was hard not to accept that part at least of the persuasiveness of an omnipresent lurking sexuality had nothing to do with the demands of sexual continence in an African cultural climate. Perhaps reliance on the Bible prepares one for the belief that all truth is to be found in a single book. Certainly cultural relativism comes especially hard to those with a clear faith, be they missionaries, self-satisfied settlers or the German volunteer who confided to me the encapsulated verity of his three years in Cameroon: 'If the natives can't eat it, fuck it, or sell it to a vite man, zey aren't interested.'

Our destination was a desolate village at the foot of the harsh granite mountains. It seemed a miracle that anything could grow in the thin, baked soil. The difference in temperature between here and what I had come to view as 'my' end of Dowayoland was considerable and both Matthieu and I were glad to slump in the shade while our host was being sought.

He revealed himself as a short, wizened little man dressed in rags. He was very drunk indeed, although it was only ten in the morning. We went through the normal greetings; mats were brought to sit on. As I had feared, food was to be prepared. I could quite easily handle the odd Dowayo repast of yams, peanuts, even millet; unfortunately, when I turned up at a strange village, there was a social imperative to offer me meat as a sign of respect. Since no one was about to go out and slaughter a steer for the mere joy of impressing me, this normally meant smoked meat which had been suspended in the intermittent smoke above the cooking fire for an indefinite period. Once a sauce was added it released a stench that had a powerful emetic effect. Fortunately, it is impolite to watch strangers eat and so I would retire to a hut with Matthieu to dine. This enabled me to renounce all claims to the proffered food without giving offence, Matthieu eating for two of us while I crouched in a corner and tried to think of other things.

While this feast was being concocted, I began to talk to my host about inconsequential matters, asking, for example, for information on subjects I already knew about. As I had feared, the answers I received were evasive and liberally mixed with half-truths. Moreover, it seemed that there was some doubt as to whether or not the harvest was imminent. Perhaps he would be able to arrange it for tomorrow, perhaps not. Ideally, in the course of fieldwork one would have no truck with such informants but restrict one's activities to those of a polite, kindly and generous disposition who found that answering the relentless and pointless questions of an anthropological inquirer was an amusing and rewarding pursuit. Alas, such people are rare. Most people have other things to do, are easily bored, become annoyed at the inanity of their interlocutor or are concerned more to present themselves in a favourable light than to be strictly honest. For these, the best tactic is quite simply bribery. A small amount of money converts the anthropological quest into a worthwhile activity and opens doors that would otherwise remain closed. On this occasion, as on others, it worked. A small present ensured that the harvesting would be organized with minimum delay and that I should witness the whole operation from start to finish; he would go off and organize it now. As he waddled away, one of his wives arrived with an enormous dish of smoked meat.

Scarce had the last morsel of pungent flesh been swallowed than we heard the sound of slashing machetes; the millet was being cut. Matthieu whispered to me the secret of our host's eagerness to please. The poll-tax was due for payment. He would be able to use my present to discharge it and so be able to avoid sharing it with any relatives in need.

Work continued throughout the day and I sat out in the fields watching and trying desperately to talk to the workers. They and I were mutually almost incomprehensible, sad proof of how localized my knowledge of the language was. There were long, awkward silences, not improved by the Dowayo habit, when confronted by a silent stranger, of crying, 'Say something!' This quite infallibly drives all thoughts of conversation from the mind.

The men and women laboured all day, perspiration running in rivulets down their faces and chests as they stooped and slashed, the millet keeling over with a dry rustle, the multi-coloured heads toppling the ten or eleven feet to the ground. Occasionally they would break off to gulp water or smoke a cigarette with me, none being in the least annoyed at my tranquil watch, but rather concerned lest the shift in position of the sun might not trouble me and make me unpleasantly hot. There was much speculation about the size of the harvest. It might be thought that since the evidence lay before them an accurate assessment could be easily made of the yield; nothing could be further from the truth. They spoke as if the actual moment of harvest lay far in the future, as if no accurate data was available on which an opinion might be based. The way the crop fell betokened good or ill, the way the heads reached up to a man's ankle bone foretold this or that. There was great fear that witchcraft might rob them of the crop until the very last moment or deprive it of its 'goodness' so that a man might eat heartily of it yet still be hungry. To prevent such interference, the field and threshing floor where nature's foison lay heaped up were heavily protected with spines and spikes to injure marauding witchcraft. Strangely, it was not taken as an omen that two of the workers trod on bamboo-spike remedies and injured themselves. Several brothers of the 'true cultivator' were busy about a fire and muttering to each other, as I inferred, arcane secrets of magic. I sent Matthieu up to offer tobacco and find out the subject of their conversation. They were wondering what remedy I put on my hair to make it straight and fair. Did women like such hair? Why did we not leave ourselves alone and look natural, the way God had made us, with black, frizzy hair?

With some ten or fifteen workers, all brothers or sons of the organizer, the work was completed in one day and all adjourned to rest and eat. Following the noise of singing, I wandered off a couple of miles towards the mountains to watch the funeral of a woman whose body, wrapped in hides and cloth, was being carried from her husband's village to that of her father for burial. This journey would be via a path over the mountain and this, added to the Dowayos' natural fear of the dark, made them eager to leave before sundown. Having been assured that no more would happen in the fields until daylight, I allowed Matthieu to go off with them in accordance with his kinship obligations. In a magnificent red sunset, with my stomach, unfed all day, rumbling ominously, we watched the party set off in a cloud of dust, singing and capering, the body hefted on an improvised stretcher. It was dark in the valley as they climbed the hill in sunlight and disappeared. From the fields came a sudden burst of singing. Something was going on.

I never established whether my exclusion from the scene was the result of guile or misunderstanding, or what role Matthieu played in the affair. It proved to be one of those matters where the more questions one asked the fewer answers one got. As I discovered from other harvests I attended, nothing of note preceded my arrival. The men had all gathered at the threshing floor, excluding women and children. Various vegetal remedies had been placed on the pile of millet heads and all were singing a circumcision song that women must not hear. No one seemed concerned either way at my presence. The beating of the millet began. The men, some stripped naked and wearing only penis sheaths, began a slow dance as they threshed. A stick was raised with the right hand over the head, seized with the left hand and brought down on the millet. All took a step sideways and the action was repeated. Hour after hour it continued, a steady chanting followed by a dull thud as the sticks hit the millet in unison. The moon came up and rose high and still the rhythmic beating continued, millet husks flying up and adhering to the streaming bodies. Even at this time of night the heat was suffocating and radiated from the earth itself.

The next thing I knew, it was dawn. The men were still working and chanting, sustained by copious beer. I was sprawled on a rock, to the great detriment of my buttocks, and leaning against a thorn tree. The general feeling of gross crapula was rather like the hangover from a night Channel crossing. I had clearly been woken by a large goat that was pensively devouring my field notes, having already eaten the autobiography of a U-boat captain with which I had been passing the time. Luckily I had acquired the Dowayo habit of hanging my possessions on trees and a quick check revealed that the only other damage was a half-eaten shoelace. Having peremptorily dismissed the goat, I rejoined the men who were now moving on to the next stage of the operation and winnowing the result of their threshing. From the sorts of jokes being bandied about, it was clear that some of them were not merely relatives but men who had been circumcised together. 'There's no wind!' cried one of the men. 'How shall we winnow? We must all fart.' He poured the grain from above his head into a basket and the chaff was blown away. The remark provoked mass hysteria, and even I was affected. The winnowing continued apace. A chicken's head was cut off over the grain and cooked wild yams called 'scorpions' food' were thrown on the heap from all directions. My host, in festive garb, was fetched from the village and piled up the grain in a basket. To this he attached a red Fulani hat and fled at great speed towards the village. When the first grain was dumped in the tall, tubular granary the crop was finally safe; witchcraft could not hurt it now.

I cannot say at what point I began to analyse the data and see how it all held together, but little by little it began to fall into place. I was sure that what I had witnessed could only be understood with reference to circumcision. I had heard enough about the ceremony to realize that the whole threshing process was conducted in the form of a story called *The beating to death of the old Fulani woman*.

An old Fulani woman had a son. He was ill. He had run in the *silkoh* grass and cut himself. His penis swelled up and was full of pus. She took a knife and cut so the child was cured. The penis became beautiful. She cut her second son. One day she went for a walk through a Dowayo village and the Dowayos saw it was good. They took circumcision and beat her to death. That was how it started because Dowayos did not know circumcision. They forbade women to see it. But Fulani women can see it. It is finished.

The beating to death is re-enacted on several occasions, most notably during the circumcision of boys. A little play is performed, whereby the old woman is depicted moaning and complaining as she walks along the road where Dowayos lie in wait for her. She passes between them twice, on the third occasion they leap up and strike the ground with sticks, cutting off the

141

leaves she is wearing. A pile of stones is set up on which are suspended the basket and red hat of the woman. The circumcision song is sung. Women and children may not be present.

The 'scorpions' food' pointed to other links. I had heard of fertility cults conducted by, among others, the rainchiefs. Before any of the crops could be brought to the village for the first time every year, certain rites must be carried out or scorpions would invade the huts and attack people. No one had hitherto mentioned to me that the scorpions that had moved into my hut were taken as a sign that I had foolishly broken this regulation in bringing supplies from outside. Throwing 'scorpions' food' on the crops leads the scorpions astray. They remain in the bush, just as throwing the excrement of the mountain porcupine at the skull ceremony would keep the dangerous ancestors clear of the village. Only much later would I learn that 'scorpions' food' was also attached to people, a girl the first time she menstruated, a boy after circumcision. It was this that later confirmed that young people on the verge of adulthood are treated like plants about to be harvested. Dowayos try to arrange that circumcision shall end with the entry of the boys to the village at the same time as the new crops are brought home. There is a common model for both.

I spent another night at the village to make quite sure that nothing else was afoot and pick up my wayward assistant who returned after dark, truly penitent. To make amends for his absence he showed me, in great secrecy, a magic stone that made pregnant women miscarry. For a successful birth they were obliged to come and offer money to the owner of the stone. His family derived a steady income from this powerful rock, but not as much as the people down the road who had one that caused dysentery. The existence of these stones was kept from the missionaries; apparently, they were held responsible for an attempt by a past French *sous-préfet* to destroy them. Dowayos were convinced that his real aim was to collect them all for himself and so become rich.

The next day we tramped back towards Kongle, the only incident on this long and very dull march being that I contrived to lose my footing while crossing a river and plunged headfirst into a deep pool, totally saturating all the films I had shot of the harvest and ruining them. This depressed me more than a little. From the material point of view, the expedition had not been a notable success; I had returned without notes or film. Still, these are, or should be, merely a means towards ideas and I had at least acquired several of those.

As a treat we called in at the mission and stayed a couple of days until mail-day. After walking around unwashed for several days, sleeping on the ground and eating skimpily, it was marvellous to sleep on a real bed, having had a shower, a proper meal – and most of all, a conversation. There was even news, a concept almost entirely alien to a seemingly timeless Dowayoland. The *sous-préfet* was leaving.

It seemed that after fourteen years in Poli he was to be replaced. By the time I reached Kongle, everyone was agog with the news. There was an atmosphere of carnival and men had gathered to drink recklessly to celebrate the departure of a man they had long regarded as an enemy. It was a golden opportunity to gather gossip; there were many eager to tell me of past wrongs. Messengers were being dispatched at intervals to town to bring back the latest news. Zuuldibo volunteered to help the old *sous-préfet* move out. Why, he would even carry his furniture on his back to the crossroads. The *sous-préfet*, I was informed, on hearing of his posting elsewhere, had come to the Dowayos and asked for magical help to have the order changed. They had smiled sweetly and told him regretfully that all their plants had died so that they could not help him. Another man came from the town. He had spoken to the *sous-préfet*'s servants through the bedroom window. His employer had made it clear that this aged retainer would receive no farewell present. The *sous-préfet* had made the man, who had hardly a shirt on his back, burn all the old clothes he would not be taking with him. This aroused great outrage. I foresaw that I should have to satisfy certain expectations when my own turn came to leave.

The stream of visitors continued, each adding his pearl of knowledge to the common pile. Lastly came Gaston, whom the Chief had dispatched on his bicycle for beer and news. He looked somewhat the worse for wear. Dowayos love to tell a story and

Gaston held the stage. Everyone settled back round the fire from which I had contrived to get as far as possible.

In Poli everyone was drunk (Zuuldibo looked envious). No one knew anything more. The *sous-préfet* had been seen packing. Gaston himself had gone to the market to see if he could pick up any information; it was full of prisoners from the jail. Poli was such an inaccessible hole that there was no possibility of their escaping, so the gaolers let them out so they could go fishing or drinking. Two of these men had been attacking a Dowayo girl when Gaston had wheeled his bicycle innocently onto the scene. 'Now you're for it!' she had shrieked, 'Here comes my husband!' At this, the two desperadoes had loosed her and set about poor Gaston; the woman made her escape, laughing. Everyone else found the story hilarious too. Gaston collapsed with mirth at his own suffering. The evening ended in uproar. Only Zuuldibo was vexed; the prisoners had stolen his beer.

11   The Wet and the Dry

The dry season had now truly come and the land was becoming a
parched wilderness of scrubby grass. The Dowayos also switched
to a totally different lifestyle: agriculture had ceased until the
next rains, except in the high mountains where irrigation was
possible. The men would devote themselves to drinking, weaving
and just sitting about, or to desultory hunting, the women would
fish or make baskets and pots. Young men would go off to the
cities in search of work and wickedness.

I had several projects in mind but these would have to wait for
Christmas. I knew only too well how awful it would be to sit
alone in Dowayoland at that most depressing of calendrical rites,
and had arranged with Jon and Jeannie to join them at the mission
at N'gaoundere. Here we enjoyed a simple but refreshing
Christmas, rather more religious than most of my markings of
this event, but alternately restful and frenetic. Walter was at his
most manic, throwing himself into the festival with an energy
worthy of a better cause. Hangovers were liberally exchanged
and we somehow contrived to forget that outside the snow was
not deep and crisp and even. There were, of course, poignant
moments. One sturdy expatriate burst into tears when ice-cream
was produced; another was visibly moved by a Christmas cake
with dried mangoes and bananas in it. I mysteriously developed
an attack of malaria after exposure to flashing Christmas lights
but was back, revictualled and revitalized after a week, to push
forward the building of my house.

This was an extremely onerous task. At one moment the earth
was too wet, a week later too dry. There was no barrel to put
water in. The grass for the roof was not ready. The man who
should be directing the job was ill, or on a visit, or wanted more
money. The contract was renegotiated with lavish histrionics

145

three times. Unless I paid more, I alone would be the cause of starving children, weeping wives, unhappy men. After several weeks of this I did what a Dowayo would have done and asked the Chief to convene a court at which my case would be arbitrated.

Dowayo courts were open to all, though women and boys would be well advised to remember their place before the elders. They would assemble beneath the tree in the public circle before the village and the *palabre* would begin. Each would state his grievances in high rhetorical style, witnesses would be called and questioned by anyone who felt like it. The Chief had no power to impose his verdict, but both parties were made well aware of public opinion and would often accept his mediation. The alternative was to take the case to Poli where it would be decided by outsiders and where there was a risk of being sentenced to prison for troubling the administrators.

Being inexperienced in the subtleties of language and procedure, I merely introduced the case myself in a speech Matthieu had rehearsed me in. It ended, 'I am but a small child among the Dowayos. I give my case to Mayo who will explain it.' This went down rather well and Mayo was able to depict my adversaries as heartless villains, taking advantage of my lack of kinsmen and my good nature to cheat me. Arguments went back and forth with myself rocking on my heels and muttering, 'It is so. It is good,' at regular intervals. Finally, I agreed to pay about twice the normal rate for the work and everyone was satisfied. It is important to note that in doing so I was not allowing myself to be cheated. A rich man expects to pay more for everything; it would be unfair if he refused to. With this in mind I did most of my purchasing through Matthieu. Doubtless he availed himself of the opportunity to take commission, but I still ended up a nett gainer. The result was that my fine house with attached garden and shady patio cost me £14.

Another case that day was typical of the functioning of Dowayo courts. The matter in hand was the dispute between an old man and a youth over a sack of millet. The man claimed that the boy had stolen the millet from his granary; the boy denied this. The old man had broken into the boy's hut to recover his goods and found only the sack which he identified as his. The two parties began to insult each other. This was too much for a Dowayo audience. Gleefully they joined in, shouting ever sillier insults: 'You have a pointed anus.' 'Your wife's cunt smells like old fish.' Finally everyone burst out laughing, including the litigants.

A man claimed to have seen the boy enter the man's granary, but he was not present. The case was adjourned until his evidence could be heard. At the next session the boy and witness were present, the old man was not; anyway, the witness had seen nothing. At the next session an ordeal was proposed. The boy would pluck a stone from boiling water and the hand would be bound up; if after a week it had healed, he would be vindicated and entitled to compensation from the accuser. The old man refused to allow it. The boy now claimed compensation for the door of his hut. The old man denied breaking it; the boy had done it to spite him. Witnesses were called and again the matter was adjourned. At the next session the witnesses were there but neither of the litigants turned up. The case simply died on its feet. The two parties never seemed to bear each other any ill will.

The law court was regarded as a form of popular entertainment and Dowayos did not hesitate to use it for the most trivial matters. I only made one other appearance in a case brought by a local man against me.

Anthropological works are full of accounts of how the fieldworker fails to 'find acceptance' until one day he picks up a hoe and begins to dig himself a garden. This immediately opens all doors to him; he is 'one of the local people'. The Dowayos are not like that. They were always appalled when I attempted the smallest act of physical labour. Should I want to haul water, frail old ladies would insist on carrying the jar for me. When I tried to make a garden, Zuuldibo was horrified. Why should I wish to do such a thing? He himself never touched a hoe; he would find a man to do it for me. So I acquired a gardener. The man had a garden by the river and so would be able to grow vegetables throughout the dry season. He refused to discuss payment; I should decide afterwards whether the work had been well done and fix a reward. Dowayos often use this technique to oblige the patron to be generous. I gave him some seeds friends had sent me: tomatoes, cucumbers, onions and lettuce. He would plant a little of each and see what would grow.

I quite forgot about the matter until I received word in late January that my garden was ready and that I should visit it. It was an extremely hot day, even for the season, and fogged by heat-haze. The earth was scorched a dark brown and seamed with deep cracks. But there, after some two miles' trek into the bush, was a pocket of bright green. As we grew closer we could see that it was a series of terraces built into the river bank. It had obviously involved a great deal of work. The wet season would clearly wash it away so that the gardener would have to begin the whole enterprise again next year. The gardener appeared and insisted on watering the crop with great expenditure of effort and lavish gestures of brow-wiping just to make sure that the amount of labour involved in such a climate was not lost on me. He explained how he had collected black earth and goat droppings and transported them out to his plot, how he had watered the shoots lovingly three times a day and protected them from animals. It was true that the carrots had been eaten by locusts and that the onions had fallen prey to the cattle of nomadic Fulani, but he had protected the lettuce. There they stood, three thousand heads of lettuce, all planted on the same day and due to mature in about a week. All this, he explained with an expansive gesture, was mine! I must confess to being somewhat taken aback by my sudden emergence as lettuce king of North Cameroon. There was no possibility of beginning to cope with such an abundance of greenery. I did not even have any vinegar.

In the next few weeks I ate more lettuce than anyone should ever be asked to. I supplied it to the mission; the bureaucrats of Poli feasted on it; bemused Dowayos received it as gifts and fed it to their goats as unfit for human consumption. I had tried to persuade the gardener to sell it in town but he met with scant success. In the end we fell out as to how much I should pay him. Since I had originally conceived of the garden as an economy measure that would add variety to my diet, I was more than a little disgruntled. I had offered the gardener 5,000 francs for the part of the crop I could eat. He could keep the rest and ell it in town. He had insisted on 20,000 francs and would not budge.

The case went to court and the lettuce grew, went to seed and rotted. Following Mayo's advice on correct legal procedure, I had supplied the chief with six bottles of beer to help him in his deliberations; my adversary would do likewise.

The case was rehearsed at length under the central tree. I stuck to my point that the crop was useless to me and that the gardener had never been asked to grow three thousand heads of lettuce but merely to try a little of each packet of various sorts of seed. My opponent stuck firmly to the point that he should be rewarded for all the work of the garden regardless. We repeated ourselves to the point of exhaustion. Finally the chief intervened; I should offer to pay 10,000 francs. Having learned the lesson that one should never agree too swiftly to anything, I hummed and haa'd and finally agreed, saying that I did not wish the gardener to be sad. The gardener reluctantly accepted, saying that he did not wish me to be sad, but said he would give me back half the money to show his pleasure at my generosity. So he ended up with the sum I had offered in the first place. Honour was satisfied all round, everyone seemed happy, but I was never quite sure I had understood what had been happening and no one seemed able to explain it to me.

My involvement with the courts suggested the possibility that reports of law cases might provide useful historical background. I had read some of those published in old colonial periodicals while still in England and they had proved most informative. The only place where such material might be available was the *sous-préfecture* in Poli. I was curious to see the new *sous-préfet* and it would doubtless be politic to seek him out and introduce myself. I trekked into town in the company of the village schoolmaster.

This gentleman was a young Bamileke, a dynamic and entre-preneurial tribe of the South-West sometimes referred to as 'the Jews of Cameroon': wherever there is industry, profit and trade, they will be found. They are dominant in many of the professions and form the backbone of the teaching staff in the North, where they are posted as a form of national service to an underdeveloped area. The teacher had formed the habit of dropping by my hut in mid-morning for a cup of coffee during school break. His conversation would consist of variations on a single theme – the horrific primitiveness of the North. 'These people are like children,' he explained. 'You clean them up, dress them, teach them right from wrong and, of course, they find it hard. They cry. But afterwards they feel better for it. That's what we Southerners do in the North.'

He would expatiate for hours on the need to teach them how to think logically which, naturally, required that they learn French. Sometimes he would tell me stories of the fighting in the South against the French and calmly recount how he had aided in the murder of a white schoolteacher by his relatives – all this as we sat quietly sipping coffee.

The new *sous-préfet* was a small, dapper little man in Fulani robes with decorative scars cut deep into his cheeks. The Dowayos called him *buuwiilo*, 'the Black White Man'. Already a sense of change had come over the town. The administrative building was being repaired, the new palace was inhabited. In the market, traders were being obliged to use scales to sell goods and prices were displayed. Most astonishing of all, the road had been repaired and a regular bus service had begun with the cities. He was a new broom determined to sweep clean.

The Black White Man welcomed me cheerfully and we had a long chat about his plans for the area. He spoke excellent French and had travelled widely in Europe. He was determined to civilize the Dowayos, which meant turning them into Frenchmen, as he himself had been turned into a Frenchman. It was noticeable that when we were interrupted by Fulanis on business, he insisted on speaking French to them. He would be delighted to have someone look through the law reports for me; I could even take them away with me. I was amazed. Never before or since did I receive such co-operation from a government official.

We parted on the best of terms and he promised to come and look me up in my village as he was making a point of visiting every part of his territory to see for himself what was going on. I scarcely took that seriously, not expecting any official to venture away from the comforts of his residence; but I was wrong. He did indeed come and see me, and toured round the village asking some very sharp questions indeed. The Dowayos were terrified. The presence of a Fulani official was about as welcome as the visit of an ancestor. As he left, he indicated the village with an expression of beatific optimism: 'Just think. In a few years all this will have given way before progress. Already things are getting better. Why, today I bought lettuce in the market. Someone has started growing it.' I managed to mumble something noncommittal. It seemed a shame to crush such a rare bloom as faith in the future.

To a Westerner it is truly striking how many of the attitudes of Africans are those that have been discarded in the West. Any colonial administrator of the nineteen-forties would agree with the opinions of my Bamileke schoolteacher or Fulani *sous-préfet*, though the two Africans would doubtless reject the comparison. Faith in that ill-defined notion, 'progress', the certainty that natives were characterized by stubbornness and ignorance and had to be forced into the present for their own good, tied them to those earnest imperialists.

Not only the 'good' parts of imperialism linger on; the 'bad' parts are there too. The economic exploitation in the name of development and the crass racialism and brutality are typical components of the scene. They are doubtless as truly indigenously African as anything can be. There is no need to accept the romantic liberal's view that all that is good in Africa comes from native traditions, all that is bad from the legacy of imperialism. Even educated Africans find themselves unable to accept that it is possible to be both black and a racist, though they still possess what we would call slaves and spit on the floor to clean their mouths after uttering the mere name of the Dowayos. The double standard was neatly exemplified by one college student with whom I was discussing the massacre of whites in Zaire. It served them right, he maintained; they were racists. You could tell they were racists as they were all white. Did that mean that he would take a Dowayo woman as his wife? He looked at me as if I were insane. A Fulani could not marry a Dowayo. They were dogs, mere animals. What had that to do with racism?

The Fulani were eager to dissociate themselves from the negroid peoples surrounding them. They had heard of a South

American people called the Bororo; this they connected with the name applied generally to the nomadic Fulani, the Mbororo. It was clear proof that Fulanis hailed from South America and had merely colonized these inferior races. Several young men offered me this theory worthy of a Thor Heyerdahl. It explained their light skin and long, non-frizzy hair, their straight noses and thin lips. They were often at great pains to point out that my exposed parts, brown from the sun, were the same colour as theirs, pale from wear.

The dry season development that most delighted the Dowayos was the arrival of my fridge. I had long sought to buy a paraffin refrigerator, regarding them wistfully in the city shops, but they cost more than I could afford and the difficulty of transporting them put the whole matter out of the question. In the abandoned house of the Dutch linguists who had worked on the language of the Dowayos there lingered such a machine. One day I had the good fortune to bump into them at N'gaoundere and they offered to lend it to me. I could not believe my luck; I should have cold water and fresh meat. My reliance on tinned food would be reduced; and some of the pressure on my finances would be relieved. I set it up outside my fine new house, the roof of which was just being completed. It was considered a great joke when I asked why they had left off the normal spikes that protect a house-dweller against witchcraft. Everyone knew that a white man was not subject to attacks from witchcraft just as everyone knew that he must live in a square, not a round house. My own house was consequently built square and, instead of witchcraft remedies, an empty beer bottle was placed on top.

To celebrate, Jon and Jeannie came out and we drank cold beer with an ecstatic Zuuldibo. My 'cold granary' was a source of great wonder to everyone. It baffled them – as it rather did me – how a fire in my 'granary' made it cold. I could not resist the temptation of showing them ice, which none but the greatest sophisticates had previously encountered. They were terrified. Never having experienced such extreme temperature difference, Dowayos would insist that ice felt 'hot'; if they touched it, it would burn them. I never fully convinced them that it was merely water in another form. Watching it melt in the sun, they would say, 'The cold matter has gone away. Only the water inside is left.' Even the Old Man of Kpan was obliged to come and see this wonder, in accordance with his role of keeper of arcane mysteries.

This enabled me to re-establish contact with him and remind him of his promise that I might visit him. The trip was arranged for the following week. His son would come to guide us.

To my great surprise, the boy arrived on the appointed day and Zuuldibo insisted on accompanying us. The trek was enlivened, as we approached the daunting mountains for the first time, by encounters with mountain dwellers. I was amused to note that the women here greeted me as their 'lover'. It was explained to me that this was a peculiarity of the area and much play was made of it. Having crossed the long, hot plains, dotted with salt-licks where wild beasts and cattle sought sustenance side by side, we began the climb. Temperatures at this time of year could be well over 110°F at noon, and both Matthieu and I were soon bathed in sweat. I had brought drinking water which he piously declined, but he was unable to avail himself of the only stream we passed since – as I have mentioned – highland water is forbidden to lowland Dowayos unless offered by a local resident. The Old Man's 'son' turned out to be some sort of a cousin and was not empowered to make the offering. The path climbed steadily through patchy trees. At whatever time of year one travelled, it was at grave risk to life and limb. In the wet season one could hang on to vegetation while clambering up rock-faces, but the ground was covered with grass and occasionally one foot would simply shoot off into space as the path became a dotted line on the cliff wall. In the dry season one could see the surface and better place the feet, but there were no handholds to rectify a mistake.

We shared our journey with jibbering baboons who sent loose shale cascading down on us from above. Beneath was a sheer drop of three hundred feet or more to a river which hissed through granite boulders. We all laughed nervously when Zuuldibo remarked on his fear of falling as he did not know how to swim. After several hours' rough passage we came out on a plateau with fantastic views over the whole of Dowayoland and away towards Nigeria. Just when I thought it would be all plain sailing, the mountainside became fissured with deep clefts. Crossing these involved quite simply leaping across the chasm and clinging to the dirt on the other side until you had regained your balance.

Finally, we emerged in a cool green valley, abundantly watered by a brook that seemed to flow from the very summit itself. At the bottom nestled a fairly large compound – the home of the rainchief. We were greeted by a number of young women, wives of the Old Man, who clucked and fussed over us. Did we want to sit outside? – inside? Would we eat? Would we take water or beer? Did we like drink cold like white men or warm like Dowayos? The Old Man was in a distant field treating a sick woman; he would be brought. We sat for perhaps an hour, chatting and dozing and then word came that, when the messenger arrived to tell him of our coming, he found that the Old Man had already set off for Poli by another path. I was convinced that this was a put-up job but had to accept it with good grace. On the mountain Matthieu and I could not hope to catch up with even an aged montagnard; pursuit was therefore out of the question. Zuuldibo, who had been dozing, announced that he had dreamt that one of his cows was ill and would therefore have to return to check whether this was true or whether it was simply the spirit of an ancestor playing tricks on him. We were obliged to go back down the mountain.

This marked the beginning of my campaign to win over the rainchiefs and persuade them to share their secrets with me. All 'experts' – missionaries, administrators and the like – were convinced that the stubborn unreasonableness of the Dowayos would ensure that I got nothing out of them. I confess that I thought so too.

However, I began a policy of visiting them all, one by one, of asking them to visit me when they passed through Kongle, and of shamelessly playing off one against the other. I pretended to the rainchief of Mango that I had only come to him in the hope that he might be able to tell me something about the real rainchief at Kpan. When I next saw the Old Man of Kpan, I confessed that I had erroneously once considered him to be a rainchief but had learned that he really knew little about it. Perhaps he could tell me, however, about what happened at Mango? Since these two were great rivals, the shaft hit home. On one occasion, when the Old Man of Kpan passed through Kongle, he was told that I had gone to Mango for two days. He finally broke, and I began a series of visits to him. On the first occasion he confessed that his father had been a rainchief and that he had asked around on my behalf and found out one or two very general points about the techniques involved. I was careful to be effusive in my thanks and to reward him generously even though my finances were once more in dire straits.

Over the next six months I trekked up his mountain six or seven times. Each time, he failed quite to live up to his promises, but told me just a little more. Each little detail he let slip I could use to talk to people from my village; they assumed that I knew more than I did and let slip a little more still. A golden opportunity came when Mayo developed a feud with the Old Man over non-payment of brideprice. He intoned a great denunciation of the rainchief and all his works, listing his past misdeeds, killing people with lightning, destroying fields with porcupines, etc. He was not afraid of the Old Man even if he caused a drought. He pointed out to me the various mountains involved in rainmaking, their differential importance and what sorts of stones caused various varieties of rain. By the time he and the Old Man were reconciled, I had a pretty good idea of the whole complex. It was crucial, however, to verify my information and try to witness the operations themselves since it was the focus of several areas of symbolism concerning sexuality and death.

Several events helped bring us together. The rainchief was mooted to be the man who had the magic plant called *zepto* that cured male impotence. This was in no way refuted by his own affliction by this complaint as noised abroad by his thirteen wives and confirmed in the private investigations conducted by my friend Augustin among the unsatisfied ladies of Dowayoland. The Old Man of Kpan asked me whether white men did not have roots to cure impotence. I replied that I had indeed heard of such things but could not say whether they worked. This reply pleased him greatly, marking me out as a 'man of straight words'. Through the offices of a sex-shop in London I managed to purchase a quantity of Ginseng in a lavishly illustrated bottle and gave it to him as all I could offer in this direction. The only upshot was a case of diarrhoea. He did not take this ill, however, agreeing that even the best remedies sometimes went wrong. He shook his head sagely, 'There are no remedies that make an old field new,' he remarked.

Another incident that did much to cement our solidarity was an extraordinary visit by the new *sous-préfet* later in the year. As part of his modernization of the Dowayos, he came to announce that Dowayo cattle sacrifices must cease and that circumcision must be limited to the school holidays. A large party of officials and bureaucrats had driven out in a fleet of cars from Poli and held court under a huge tree. One after another, they gave impassioned speeches forbidding this or that. The Dowayos nodded solemnly and covertly grinned at one another. The Bamileke schoolteacher had prepared himself in advance for this visit, clearly having been tipped off by someone. He took the opportunity of denouncing the people of the village for their slothful and barbarous ways. For years they had promised him a new school but had put off building one. Whenever he returned after the holidays, he discovered that furniture and parts of the building had been removed. I shifted uneasily at this point, knowing that parts of my house had been previously incarnated in the sagging roof of his classroom. The Old Man of Kpan, crouching to one side, began to give me 'significant' looks and nod towards the mountains. This was right at the end of the dry season and although there were clouds everywhere, no rain had as yet fallen. But there, over by the mountains, some eight or nine miles away, rain was falling. The *sous-préfet* began a long oration about the value of education. The people here should take advantage of it and their favoured status as an underdeveloped area. The rain drew nearer. The schoolmaster, encouraged by favour from on high, presented a list of the names of parents who had been keeping their children away. Here was a second list, containing the names of parents who sent their children with no other sustenance but the traditional midday food – beer. The result was that the children were drunk all afternoon. At the moment he handed over the list, a squall of great power engulfed the entire party. Complaining and cursing, they all melted into their cars and disappeared back to town. We all fled to our huts. Both the rainchief and the schoolmaster ended up in mine and we drank coffee to warm ourselves up. 'Did you see that?' cried the Bamileke. 'These people! There are sorcerers here. Someone called that storm to stop me. These people won't be helped.'

Matthieu muttered a simultaneous translation in Dowayo in the rainchief's ear. He and I chuckled. I had a long argument with the schoolmaster denying the possibility of anyone making it rain, the very existence of sorcerers, the impotence of magic; he defended all these beliefs earnestly. The rainchief sniggered more and more and finally became red in the face from hysteria.

When the schoolmaster left I asked the Old Man whether he had made it rain. He turned on me a look like a cherubic tortoise. 'But only God makes it rain.' He collapsed in laughter, mightily pleased with the day's work. 'But if you come and see me next week I'll show you how I help God.'

By now, the rainmaker had told me most of what I was to learn about rainmaking. It depended ultimately on the possession of certain special stones, like those that maintained the fertility of cattle and plants. It was to be many months before I actually saw these in their secret cave up under the waterfall. Each time I was promised that next time it would happen. It was, alas, impossible on this occasion because it was still the dry season and to approach the stones might cause a flood, or because it was the wet season and we might be struck by lightning, or because one of the women was menstruating and thus dangerous to the stones. With thirteen wives around, there was hardly a time when one of them was not menstruating.

For the time being, the rainchief showed me his portable rain kit. Once he had started the rainy season with the special stones on the mountain, he could cause localized downpours with the contents of a hollow goat's horn. He took me off into the bush and we crouched down behind a rock with much extravagant looking round and scanning of the horizon. Inside was a plug of ram's wool. 'For clouds,' he explained. Then came an iron ring. This served to localize the effect of the rain: if, for example, he were at a skull-festival, he would make it rain in the middle of the village until the people brought him beer. Next came the most powerful part of all. This was a great secret that he had never shown anybody. He bent forward earnestly and tipped up the horn. Slowly, there rolled forth into his hand a child's blue marble such as one might purchase anywhere. I made as if to pick it up. Horrified, he withdrew his hand: 'It would kill you.' I questioned him about it. Was it not from the land of the white men? Certainly not; it had come from the ancestors many thousands of years ago. How did this stone make it rain? You rubbed ram's grease on it. This was interesting, since human skulls also had to be rubbed with grease before being placed in the bush. I began to suspect that skulls, pots and stones were all related in a single complex. This in fact proved to be the case, the rainchiefs being the cross-over point from one area to another. Rainchiefs' skulls cause rain and are often replaced with water-jars for festivals, while the mountain on which the rainstones are kept is called 'The crown of the boy's head'. In other words, mountains are treated as if they were the 'skulls of the earth'. Once again, a single model centred on stones and skulls was being used to structure many areas and bring rainfall and human fertility into relationship with each other.

I thanked and rewarded the Old Man, and Matthieu and I descended the mountain in pensive silence. When I returned to the village my fine fridge had stopped working, spoiling several weeks' supply of meat. Hereafter it never worked properly again, seeming to know when I was not about to keep it in order. The moment my back was turned it would extinguish itself and simmer its contents to advanced putrescence in hours. Several times I returned to find Dowayos literally in tears before the 'cold granary', weeping at the waste of food, unable to relight the apparatus but resolute that they could not touch the contents as they did not belong to them. I soon relegated it to the status of a mere cupboard. 'West Africa wins again,' declared Herbert Brown delightedly.

Up on the rainchief's mountain I had conceived a plan. Jon and Jeannie had offered me a lift to N'gaoundere the next day on a supplies trip so I could put it into practice at once. Stopping only to jettison my rotten meat and change my shirt, I set off for the

mission. Three days later I was back in the rainchief's village. By
a subtle combination of cajoling and bribery, I had weaned from
Walter's children a single blue marble that I bore triumphantly
back with me.

'You recall the stone you showed me?'

'Yes.'

'I asked you if it was from the land of the white men.'

'Yes.'

'Is it the same as this one?' I handed him the marble. With a
gasp he examined it against the light.

'It is the same. The clouds in it are darker.'

'Would this stone cause rain?'

He regarded me with amazement. 'How can I know? I would
have to try it, to see if it would work. I cannot tell you until I
have seen it.' He shook his head, clearly puzzled that I would
expect him to make statements not founded upon direct experience.

It was not until my very last week in Dowayoland that I was
finally allowed to visit the magic mountain itself. Having little
time left, I felt that a final all-or-nothing attempt to prove the
mysteries was in order. I announced that I would visit him on a
certain day to say goodbye, glad to be making the perilous trip
for the very last time. When we arrived the village was totally
silent; the women had been sent away. We talked for a little
while. Would my wives have sown my millet when I arrived back
at my village? Did my father have many cattle? Would the rains
have started? This was my cue. Matthieu had carefully rehearsed
me in a little speech of thanks mingled with hurt reproach. I was
grateful that he had talked to me but my heart was sad that I
would return to the land of the white men without ever having
seen the rainstones. This had to be put in rather a more ornate
style to be acceptable in Dowayo. 'It is like a little boy,' I ad
libbed, 'walking with his father. His father says to him, "Do not
be tired. When we reach the mountains, I shall carry you." But
when they arrive there, the father does not keep his word. "Do
not be sad," says the father, "when we are half-way up, I shall
carry you." But when they reach this point, the father does not
keep his word . . .' The Old Man took the point and clapped my

159

little performance. He had guessed that I would be sad and had decided that I could be trusted not to repeat foolishly before women what I would see. We would go to the rainstones. Matthieu began to roll his eyes and begged me not to go: I should be killed. I reminded him that white men cannot be struck by lightning. The Old Man told me to take all my clothes off and he did likewise. He chewed up special plants. I recognized the aromatic smell of *geelyo* as he spat them all over me and rubbed them on my chest. I had to put on a penis sheath but as a concession to my 'supple skin' was allowed to keep my boots on. I was warned not to talk or make sudden movements and to touch nothing. Off we went.

The slope was very steep and we slithered about on the loose rock. The Old Man was chuckling, obviously having a splendid time; I was somewhat less at my ease, being concerned for my camera and suffering much from the thorns that dotted the escarpment. Finally we arrived at a point just below the summit, at a height of two thousand metres. It was bitterly cold. A watercourse issued from above and beneath the icy spray was a hollow in the rock. Within were large, lumpy clay pots like waterjars; inside these were stones of various colours for male and female rain. The Old Man splashed them with the same remedies he had spat on me and held the rocks out for my inspection. There was one more thing. We splashed through the water to a large, white rock. This was the ultimate defence of the Dowayos. If he removed this the whole world would be flooded and all would be killed.

We returned at breakneck speed, grateful for the comparative warmth of the valley, washed and dressed. The Old Man settled back in his hut. He had shown me everything. He had explained the various sorts of rain, how to make the rainbow by rubbing red ochre on a sickle and revealed the location of the rainpots. Was I happy? I was indeed very happy and rewarded him for his revelations. There was one thing more: I had not actually seen him make it rain. Would he now do so?

He smiled indulgently. Had I not seen the remedies he had splashed on the stones? It would rain between here and Poli. We should now go down the mountain before dark. Darkness did not bother him, of course, he remarked, hinting at his rumoured ability to turn into the nocturnal leopard.

The storm hit us at the very worst point of the descent where we were executing goat-like leaps across the fissures. Granite becomes very slippery when wet. At one point I was reduced to crawling on all fours. The Old Man was sniggering and pointing to the sky. Had I now seen? We were shouting above the storm to be heard. 'That's enough,' I cried, 'you can make it stop.' He looked at me with a twinkle in his eye. 'A man does not take a wife to divorce her the same day,' he replied.

Matthieu and the rainchief were both cock-a-hoop about the tempest. I, of course, would never believe anything so against the grain of my own culture without much better evidence than this. I – like they – see what I expect to see. The anthropologist in the field is seldom troubled by the 'false' beliefs of those about him; he simply puts them in brackets, sees how they all fit together and learns to live with them on a day-to-day basis.

Mariyo was delighted by our dilapidated condition when we returned to Kongle. The renowned impotence of the rainchief and his possession of so many wives led her to draw certain conclusions about my eagerness to climb the mountain – especially since the Old Man was so often away when I called. She had taken to calling me 'my lover' after the fashion of the mountain women. As an alternative outlet for my baser passions, she had invented a fat Fulani woman I kept in Garoua with a ring through her nose. This huge Fulani woman assumed mythic proportions; she was so fat that she had to be transported on a truck; she was incapable of walking without leaning on servants. In the dry season, I and my kinsmen would sit in her shade.

I avenged myself by inquiring after the old Koma man who enjoyed her favours. Every tribe had someone to despise. For the Dowayos, the Koma fulfilled this very necessary function. A pagan tribe some thirty odd miles away across the river, the Koma were credited with a debased form of language by the Dowayos; they were savages who lived in incredible squalor, horribly primitive. Their ugliness was a standing joke among the Dowayos.

Whenever I gave Mariyo a present I pretended that it had been left for her by her aged Koma, whom I had been able to understand very well as all his teeth had fallen out with age but he had led me to believe that this was in payment for sexual services. I described at length the costume of burial cloth she had made for him. Since he was so near death, they would not have to wrap his corpse but could tumble him directly into a grave in his outfit. On one occasion I captured a stick-insect and kept it for her, pretending I thought it was her shrivelled-up old Koma come to visit her. Whenever she looked tired, this was imputed to the efforts of her paramour when she went to fetch water; we both knew this was a mere excuse to rendezvous with her lover in the bush. These sessions did much to relieve the tedium of village life and were a major factor in the creation of such 'acceptance' as was granted me by the Dowayos.

Being themselves sexually active, the Dowayos were truly baffled by my asexual life and the men would always ask me about it. How did I survive? Why did I not become ill? There are two basic models of sexual relations in Africa. In one, women are weakening and dangerous to a man, robbing him of his essential virility; in the other, his sexuality feeds on them. The more he fornicates, the stronger he becomes.

Rather to my surprise in view of their notions of male 'closure' in the practice of circumcision, the Dowayos opted for the latter model. They found my ability to live without a wife truly mysterious and compared it to the habits of the Catholic fathers who lived asexually but in the company of nuns. The priests had wisely insisted on calling these not 'sisters' – since sisters are to Dowayos simply any woman of the same age – but 'mothers' with whom sexual relations are not permitted. The rumours of my vastly raunchy expeditions to the city were soon established and lent credence to Mariyo's jokes. Since one of my principal occupations on such trips was the search for spare parts for equipment that had fallen foul of pervasive African entropy, the expression 'I'm going to the city for parts' rapidly acquired a salacious ring between Jon and myself. Alas, actual journeys bore little resemblance to these orgies of the collective imagination. Sexual encounters in Africa are so unromantic and brutish in their nature that they serve rather to increase the alienation of the fieldworker, not to moderate it, and are best avoided. I know from informal conversations with colleagues that such is not always the case. The sexual position of the fieldworker has undergone a radical revision in line with changes in the sexual mores of the West. Whereas in the colonial era other races were not permitted as sexual partners – like those of different social class or religion – nowadays lines are much less clear cut. It is astonishing how many lone females were able to wander around unmolested among 'savage' peoples largely because, for the natives too, they did not figure on the sexual map. Nowadays, however, things have changed and the solitary female is almost required to engage in sexual relations with her people as part of new ideas of 'being accepted'. Any unaccompanied female who returns inexperienced tends to excite surprised and almost reproachful comment among fellow students. An opportunity for research has been neglected.

For the male, of course, passing opportunities arise and are often less awkward as being institutionalized on a commercial basis. This is a whole area – like the ethnographic assistant – that is absent from the anthropological literature but not the anthropological experience. The fieldworker may well decide that the whole thing is best avoided on the grounds of the huge complications it would cause in his domestic and personal life, but the problem must surely arise for all marooned for long periods in an alien culture. In my own case, being viewed by Dowayo men as having no sexual existence in the village was a considerable blessing; I was allowed all manner of freedoms that no Dowayo male would be permitted. For a man to be alone in a hut with a woman is normally taken as sure proof of flagrant adultery; but to imagine me fornicating with Dowayo maids was frankly farcical, and I for one was glad that this was so.

Problems about my precise nature and status also troubled the police. Matters came to a head towards the end of the dry season. Firstly, there was the incident of the irregular helicopter. A Swiss mission organization, vastly endowed with funds, had decided in its wisdom that the pagan montagnards could best be converted by a pastor descending upon them by helicopter in their remote fastnesses. Certainly the effects must have been dramatic. One day, when I was at the mission, this machine descended from on high and hovered above, emitting a loud bellowing noise: clearly it was the intention to summon someone to the local landing strip. Since I was the only one about who could drive, I borrowed a car and set off. The helicopter contained two rather bemused divines from N'gaoundere looking for Herbert Brown who had left that morning for N'gaoundere by road. They were trying to spot his car from the air. In a swirl of dust they were aloft and gone at precisely the moment when a truckload of gendarmes, armed to the teeth, turned up to arrest the 'smugglers from Nigeria' that had been reported as landing. I was hauled out of the car. Where was their landing permit, their flight plan, pilot's licence? My protestations of baffled ignorance clearly cut little ice. I was unable to say precisely who was aboard or what they were doing, or give the registration number of the aircraft. My unwillingness to swear that the aircraft had never at any time been closer than ten miles to the border was taken as incontrovertible proof of smuggling activities. It took some time to disengage myself and re-establish my credentials as a harmless idiot.

No sooner had this blown over than there was more trouble. One evening I set off for the local hospital to visit a man from my village who had been bitten by a snake. My torch being defective, I soon got lost in the maze of footpaths that surrounded the town and was thankful, after half an hour's blundering around in total darkness, to see a light ahead. I made for it and was amazed to find myself behind the house of the *sous-préfet*'s assistant. Pausing to explain myself to a lounging youth at the gate, I regained the main street.

Two days later, as I was working with the potters, Jon and Jeannie turned up in Kongle: the gendarmes had been round asking about me. An official-looking document summoned me to the police station for an identity check. Having assured myself that baking of the pots would not happen till the next day, I set off with them to town. The needle-chewing commandant took me to his office and we spent half an hour or so working out who I was and what precisely I was doing in Poli. This was accompanied by many hooded looks and significant stares. I began to be anxious.

It seemed that I was accused of taking a photograph of the back wall of the house where the *sous-préfet*'s assistant lived. This constituted 'strategic information'. Witnesses had been found who swore that I had had a camera in my hand when found skulking around the house. How often did I go to Nigeria? My denials were brushed aside; there were witnesses. Did I know it was an offence to cross the border? I had been seen. This continued for some time until I was released with a stern warning that my behaviour would be watched. The obsession of Third World countries with spying is a constant menace to the field-worker, only partly explicable by actual cases of research in sensitive areas being financed by interested parties. The real problem lay in my total inability to explain to someone who had no conception of pure research why a foreign government should be interested in an isolated tribe of mountain renegades. It was quite clear to the police chief that the only reasonable explanation lay in the nearness of the Nigerian border. Hence I was either a smuggler or a spy preparing the way for invasion. Quite what the value of a photograph of the back wall of the *sous-préfet*'s assistant's house would have been in all this was never explained.

Only much later, when I came to know him better, did the *sous-préfet* tell me that he had been keeping an eye on things and would have protected me from his over-zealous gendarmes; he had regarded the whole thing as an enormous joke. At the time my own response was one of weary disquiet which was only increased by the fact that policemen suddenly started dropping unexpectedly at my village to check where I was. This event also coincided – by chance or design – with the loss of a batch of film I had posted in Poli. Jon, as ever, was a staunch support in these troubles and took me to the mission to pour beer into me until I felt better.

12 First and Last Fruits

I had now been away from England for about a year, and while I cannot say that I felt at home in Dowayoland I seemed to have reached some sort of intermediate stage where most things had a deceptive familiarity. It was time to start tidying up my notes and attack those areas that I had put aside till greater linguistic competence and personal contacts made research more feasible. One area of special importance was the agrarian rites of fertility. These centred partly on the Old Man of Kpan, partly on his relatives I had met over the far side of Dowayoland at those first skull-festivals I had attended. They involve treating the magic stones that ensure plant fertility with special remedies. In Kpan this is collapsed with the rainmaking: the remedies are thought to 'repair the earth' by falling with the rain. At the other end of Dowayoland the rituals involve setting a line of stones across each end of the valley as a 'barrier against famine'. I now began a series of short raids into this area to talk to the holders of these secrets, the 'Masters of the Earth'.

Once again, my car being still out of action, I relied on the generosity of Jon and Jeannie for transport. Thanks to them I was able to make frequent visits to this remote area without marches of more than ten miles and without losing touch with the Old Man of Kpan. To my great surprise, the people here were quite happy to show me all the paraphernalia of their ceremonies merely on the understanding that I would say nothing of it to women. Now that everyone knew that I was working with the Old Man, they were prepared to trust me too, especially since word had circulated that I was willing to pay the necessary costs. I spent several weeks clambering about from cave to mountain and skull-house and rushing back to Kpan to wheedle further information out of the Old Man At the same time, the other rainchief at Mango sent word that he too was about to start the rainy season so I had to break off and rush up his mountain. Here, the mountain Dowayos performed the normal trick of sending us round and round in circles all day, hoping that we would get tired and go away. It is a strategy that has stood them in good stead since the arrival of the first government station in Poli. Being by now somewhat hardened to their methods, Matthieu and I paid a local to act as guide and doggedly refused to let him abandon us until we had found the rainchief, swearing that we would sleep outside his hut that night and follow him all the next day if we had to. The rainchief was soon discovered near by and proved most happy to see us; it seemed that the 'leading round the mountain' technique was merely standing orders for all outsiders. Strangely, he had heard of my difficulties with the police chief and these engendered sympathy; it appeared that he had had problems with him too.

This rainchief was a bright and cheerful young man who would quite happily have started the rainy season there and then by slaughtering a black goat and smearing the blood on the rainpots hidden out in the skull-house. His adviser, however, a piratical old man who proved to be his uncle, refused to allow it. How were they to be sure I had not been in contact with a menstruating woman? What of the Dowayos who did not expect the rain for a few weeks yet? It was when he began to question the wisdom of letting an uncircumcised man approach the pots that I knew he was simply creating difficulties. Outsiders do not have to be circumcised to be present at Dowayo rituals; even foreign women are acceptable. We began to talk about money. I devoted an hour to shaking my head and looking horrified every time he mentioned a sum. In the end we agreed on a price. For the ultimate secret of Dowayoland, I did not feel cheated to pay some £8 which gave me the right to half the goat. The affair was swiftly dispatched with none of the air of awe that would mark it at Kpan. It was hardly more dramatic than a normal goat-slaying, the beast being thrown on its back and choked by a foot pressed into its throat. When it lost consciousness, its throat was slit, the blood being collected in a gourd.

We all rushed off into the bush to a distinctly down-at-heel skull-house that contained the rainpots. These were the same as those I would see later at Kpan. The area was forbidden to strangers and we had to crawl on our bellies under thorn bushes to reach the overgrown, gloomy glade where it stood. After a perfunctory splashing about we returned to the village and began a talk that lasted several hours.

It was here that I learned perhaps the most important piece of information for the interpretation of Dowayo cultural symbolism. Previous information about rainchiefs had linked together human fertility and rainfall. The 'true cultivator's' harvest had linked together plant fertility and circumcision through the 'beating to death of the old Fulani woman'. Here I learned of links between rainfall, circumcision and plant fertility. It appeared that the day the stones were wiped clean to begin the dry season was the day the mountain, 'the crown of the boy's head', was fired for the first time (i.e. 'dried') and also the day that first fruits were brought to the village that year with the boys who had been newly circumcised. These too, I later established, were also changed from 'wet' to 'dry'. Foreskins are despised by Dowayos quite explicitly as causing a boy to be wet and smelly like a mere woman; a circumcised penis is dry and clean. When boys leave the village to be circumcised they are 'wet' and have to kneel in the river for three days. When they are cut, it will rain continuously. Only gradually can they leave the riverside camp and move out towards the mountains. Only at the dry season can they return to the village and are placed at the foot of the shrine on which the skulls of dead cattle are exposed. Here, the first fruits from the fields are flung on the same day. In other words, all the various spheres of fertility are brought together in a single system and the change from wet to dry season is tied up with the change from 'wet' uncircumcised boy to 'dry' circumcised man.

It was to take many more months of research and detailed analysis back home before the finer points of the system would be worked out, but the basic structure of all that I had witnessed and painstakingly noted in my time in the field suddenly held together and 'made sense'. 'Eureka' moments are always exciting; the fact that mine came out of the blue, up a mountain, the man giving the information having no idea of its importance to me,

ded force to my pleasure in glimpsing the structure behind all
ese rites in all its simplicity. Matthieu must have found me
rangely skittish as we came down the mountain. In my exube-
nce, I drank the cold water that came straight down from the
ountain top without bothering to chlorinate or boil it. I shall
ver know whether this was the source of my punishment for
ch hubris or whether it was some virus lurking in my liver.
hichever it was, I went down with hepatitis again.

It was when I was at my lowest ebb that Augustin and his
test of many female companions favoured me with a visit. They
nsidered my condition gravely; the disease was known to them.
he best thing is to vomit,' Augustin declared roundly. 'You
ust vomit a great deal.' His companion dissented: 'He must be
rged. Only powerful purging can remove the illness. In my
lage many die from this disease.'

'Purging is no good. He must vomit.'

'Not so. You purge until there is blood.'

The discussion went back and forth. I thanked them and noted
e various substances that would make me strain and spew to
eir satisfaction.

Some kind soul at the mission at N'gaoundere had passed on
me the secret of curing hepatitis – a decoction of guava leaves
hot water. It certainly seemed to help more than anything else.
ater I learned that a German pharmaceutical company was
sting a drug based upon just this compound. I had dispatched
Matthieu to hunt guava leaves, which are not normally found
is far north. He claimed to know of a tree in a riverside grove
me five miles away. I could scarcely believe that we were talking
out the same species but he confounded me by returning later
the day with a bag full of what indeed were guava leaves.

My condition slowly improved. The Dowayos were so im-
essed that they started treating the disease with the same
medy; so every anthropologist in some way changes the people
studies. My only other known effect was in toponymy. The
ace where my garden proved the suitability of the climate for
e cultivation of lettuce was known, years later, as 'Salad Place'.

It was during this period that the first rains of the year actually
rived. The inexorably torrid heat of the late dry season was

immediately quenched by the first downpour amid general re-joicing. I myself was somewhat less ecstatic than most since the roof of my new hut leaked like a sieve all night. I was reduced to crouching in one corner, shivering horribly, with my suitcase balanced on a ledge above my head to keep off the rain and my notes clutched in my hands. The next morning the thatcher blandly informed me that all new roofs shared this feature; it would stop after a few days. I will not claim to have believed him; I simply lacked the experience necessary to refute his assertions. The statement looked dangerously like those made by figures who had rented me leaking boats, assuring me that the wood would soon swell to make them watertight, or the Cameroonian dentist who swore to me that my gums would shrink to fit his wobbly dentures. After a miserable week of constant inundation I felt it time to invoke my guarantee of satisfaction, and repairs were undertaken. To my surprise, these consisted of simply hitting the roof with a piece of wood; to my even greater surprise, it worked.

During this time, with the neurosis of a man coming to the end of his fieldwork, I transferred my notes to the mission to preserve them from the damp, termites, goats, little boys and other menaces that my imagination conjured up.

It was while I was alone there, Jon and Jeannie being off in the bush about their business, that I was summoned to the door by loud shouting. It was the welder, an enormous fellow who revelled in the self-given name Black Buck. 'Hey, White Man,' he called 'your car just tried to kill me.' It appeared that he had been welding a section onto the car, whose existence I had tried hard to forget, when it had slipped and narrowly missed falling on him. He seemed to feel that this had occurred through some malevolence on my part.

'Are you all right?' I inquired.

'All right? Look at this.' From within his trousers he produced an enormous penis and waved it accusingly at me. The relevance of this disclosure escaped me until on closer examination a small cut was revealed for which he demanded 'urgent care'. I was frankly at something of a loss, not knowing where to lay my hands on appropriate medications. A rapid search offered

thing but concentrated bleach. Feeling that on the whole this
as not a good idea, I urged him to consult Herbert Brown, just
own the hill, as I knew he kept supplies for such emergencies.
ack Buck shuffled off, still outraged.

It was not until I had returned to my labours of classifying
tes that it occurred to me that Herbert Brown was not there,
ving gone off to repair a truck, but that his wife, a somewhat
rvous lady, was. I pictured Black Buck ambling up to the door
d exposing himself. Perhaps I should run down the hill and
tervene? But on the whole discretion seemed the better part of
lour. Since I heard no piercing scream, I assumed that Black
ck had been discreet about the area of his injury.

Being now sufficiently recovered to undertake another trek,
atthieu and I made a final outing to the western end of Do-
oyoland to see the harvest of the borassa palms. These give a
herical, coconut-like fruit that has to be treated in many ways
e a human skull, and placed on the cattle-shrine lest scorpions
ague the village. I had never seen one of these before and was
ite keen to taste them.

When we arrived at the village of the 'Master of the Earth' we
und him surrounded by this fruit, contentedly munching its
sh. It is eaten in two ways. It can be soaked in water to cause
rmination; the young shoot is then consumed and is rather like
lery. Alternatively, it can be eaten straight. The flesh is fibrous
d orange in colour; its texture is rather like a doormat, the
avour like a peach. Having chewed away manfully for some
ne, I began to get the hang of it and find it rather enjoyable. A
ndly old woman, clearly perceiving that the fruit held difficulties
r me, brought me a calabash of the flesh ready stripped. This
as very much more tender. I remarked on it to Matthieu.

'Of course, *patron*,' he replied, 'she has already chewed it for
u.'

Now that it was getting near end of term, interested parties
gan to visit me, eyeing certain of my possessions and remarking
w desperately they needed a blanket or what a nice saucepan I
d. The Chief said how much he would miss me and talked
out all the things we had done together, how much he had
joyed them though they had put him to much trouble. Matthieu

began telling me absently about the problems he was havin
buying a wife. 'You have to get them young,' he explained, 'an
form them to your will.' His intended was about twelve. 'If they'r
young, they always want money for school.' He sighed. Who di
he know who could let him have enough money to put his wif
through school? Only Mariyo seemed to think of me as anythin
but a source of material benefit; when we talked of my departur
she wept and said she would miss having me to talk to.

The whole town was abustle with the impending national fes
tival. Various attractions had been set up, and the Dowayos wer
required to produce a number of dancers to perform the ci
cumcision dance. This interested me considerably since I ha
been unable to witness circumcision itself. Years are divided int
male and female. Circumcision can only occur in a male year;
had arrived in a female year. Moreover, even after the change o
years there was not sufficient millet to feed the boys for thei
protracted stay in the bush. The festival had not been performe
for some five years and the situation was becoming a scandal.
had therefore to rely on informants' descriptions of what the
had undergone, circumcisers' accounts of how the affair wa
organized and such photographic material as I could glean fron
records and missionaries who had spent many years in Do
wayoland. The absence of this central part of Dowayo symbolisr
was not, however, as serious as it might otherwise have bee
since most other ceremonies were 'quotes' from circumcisior
reproducing exactly what happened on that occasion.

I was nonetheless glad to be able to witness the dance of th
boys before they are cut. They are decorated in burial cloth
leopard skins, animal horns and a great weight of robes an
other decorative material. Two boys who had already been ci
cumcised were obliged to undertake this uncomfortable an
rather humiliating task, since there was no time to teach younge
boys how to deport themselves. They were disgusted at the ide
and refused point blank to have anything to do with it. Zuuldib
made promises of beer and money and they reluctantly accepted
The next day he appeared at my hut asking me to reimburse hir
since, after all, the whole thing had been organized simply becaus
it would interest me.

His own generous indulgence in sloth was threatened by an
[ed]ict of the *sous-préfet*'s declaring that everyone must keep a
[ga]rden. Zuuldibo declared that it was pointless to have a garden
[un]til one had a good cactus fence around it to keep out marauding
[an]imals. He reckoned that it would be about a year before he
[co]uld tell whether the roots of the cactus had taken. Next, he
[de]clared that it was senseless to have a field unless one also had a
[hu]t in it around which beer could be offered to workers. Alas it
[w]as not the right season to build, so this too would take another
[ye]ar. On the whole, he felt that the first hoe of dirt would be
[tu]rned in about three years' time, but every morning he would
[br]avely announce that he was 'going to his field' and he would sit
[th]ere under a tree, often with me, and talk about whatever came
[in]to his head. I sometimes felt like an unpaid psychiatrist as he
[ra]mbled on about his dreams, the women he had known, the
[bu]rdens of high office.

On the day of the festival all local worthies turned up at the
[fo]otball ground. I took advantage of the occasion to harass the
[O]ld Man of Kpan who appeared in Fulani robes and carrying a
[s]word. All the other tribes had sent in dancers who stamped and
[sh]rieked in choking dust. The big men of the administration had
[p]ut on their best uniforms; the *sous-préfet*'s looked suspiciously
[li]ke that of an Air France steward. Flags were hauled up and
[d]own, the gendarmes stamped about with their most offensive
[w]eapons, party officials availed themselves of the opportunity to
[b]eat people. The national anthem was sung. A radio was solemnly
[pl]aced on a chair and saluted as the speech of the President
[ut]tered through with generous static accompaniment. Children
[p]erformed marches and played games. No one was allowed to
[le]ave before the *sous-préfet* and we all wilted visibly in the heat.
[A] large number of children accompanied by their mothers began
[to] scream, obliging them to leave early; it was rumoured the
[w]omen were deliberately pinching them. Among the few Whites
[th]e conversation centred on the slaying and mutilation of two
[m]issionaries in the North. The Americans were nervous, the
[F]rench performed extravagant displays of what had happened to
[th]e bodies, joyfully increasing their disquiet. As the sole Eng-
[li]shman it fell to me to keep a stiff upper lip; that this character

173

is inevitably slain half-way through the second reel of all o films was neither here nor there.

All beer and soft drinks in town had been commandeered b the *sous-préfet*, so I limped off to the mission to join Jon an Jeannie and wait for the evening's entertainment – a beauty cor test.

On this particular evening Poli was very much in a mood fo overstatement. People were required to express their pleasure a independence with hysteria in the streets. There was a subtl distinction made between those invited to the *sous-préfet*'s part and those who were not; the police underlined it by charging th crowd of onlookers and beating them from time to time.

The whole main street was a solid mass of people, singing dancing, shouting greetings. Many, if not most, were cheerfull drunk. Perhaps this was the occasion for which my suit had bee intended; if so, I would have melted in the heat. It being a official party, everything was extremely formal. Serried ranks o stiff, very uncomfortable chairs were drawn up. There was clearl some arcane system for their allocation according to strict rule of precedence, but whatever it was eluded me. The doctor wa there with his enormous wife. The bureaucrats were there. Th police chief stared at me pointedly; the postmaster stonily ignore me – doubtless the result of my inquiring why all mail posted i Poli arrived in England without stamps. A large number o kinsmen of the man checking invitations seemed to have turne up.

The beauty contest had been organized by the simple expedien of sending official letters to all chiefs instructing them to send certain number of young women to town on a certain day. Quit what was made of this in the hills, I shudder to think. The Fulani in former times, were in the habit of levying slaves and concubine from these people; perhaps they feared the resumption of thi system. Whatever the precise interpretation, the women had uniformly oppressed look. Many had doubtless been made t walk long distances and were decidedly travel-stained. Th Fulanis of course disdained to exhibit their own women in thi fashion, but were delighted at the opportunity to view the wome of other races. The ladies were obliged to walk, or in most case

ouch, past the spectators in a wide circle. They had the resentful
ir of goods at a slave market and stared tearfully down at the
round or glared and hissed at their tormentors. The spectators
ose to the occasion admirably with hoots of derision mingled
ith enthusiastic offers of all manner of unions short of marriage.
minor dispute broke out between those invited and the throng
hat pressed in upon them. Some had climbed into the trees for a
etter view; these fell to the lot of the party officials who shook
he trunks until they came tumbling out to tears of popular ap-
roval. After some discussion, Miss Poli was announced –
longside her Miss Poli Two and Miss Poli Consolation. The
ous-préfet's new young assistant was delegated to present each
ith a prize, embrace them modestly and dance with the winner.
he winner was clearly from way out in the hills and terrified of
he whole proceeding. She recoiled in horror when the noble
oung assistant offered his chaste embrace. When urged to dance,
he clenched her fists tearfully and refused. Embarrassed smiles
ave way to whispered threats. She stamped her feet in their new
lue plastic shoes. Two gendarmes swooped down on her and
hrew her out. The crowd cheered. The aptly named Miss Consola-
ion stepped into the breach. The party had begun.

The music consisted of a mixture of the latest Western hits and
ndless Nigerian offerings. It was my extreme misfortune to be
equired to dance with the doctor's wife during one of the latter;
: lasted about twenty minutes. We circled the floor almost in
plendid isolation as others were either overwhelmed by the heat
r dumbstruck by our graceful passage. She was a big woman
nd after some ten minutes exhibited clear signs of strain,
umping into chairs and tripping over her feet. Neither of us
vished to offend the other by giving in, so we continued to lurch
round, streaming with sweat and gasping until some kind spirit
anded us two beers. It is not easy to drink beer from the bottle
vhile dancing but we acquitted ourselves fairly creditably and
vere rewarded by cheers from the crowd.

I felt that I had made my contribution to the festivities and
ollapsed quietly in a corner, urged on to drink by the doctor
vho should have known better. The festivities continued with
opious drink and food of the burned intestines sort. About

midnight I fell into the company of two young schoolteacher from the bush, Patrice and Hubert. It was Patrice's peculiarit that, wherever he went, he bore with him a folding chair. I seemed that he had lived for a year among the Voko in the tota absence of furniture. This condition depressed him deeply, s with his friend he had gone to Garoua and bought a foldin chair from which, he vowed, he would never be parted. He eve danced with the chair until remonstrated with by the gendarm cousin who had secured him admittance. By now beer wa running low and many had switched to red wine. I knew from experience that this would not be a good idea and was quit happy to coast for a bit. Others, however, demanded more drink It seemed that there was only one source, an illegal drinking-ha at the far end of town run by a strict Muslim. A male nurse, wh was gleefully paralytic, was engaged to fetch it on his motorbike He had to be carried to the machine, being incapable of walking and roared off into the night. I could see no way that he coul even stay on the machine let alone bring back beer. However, fiv minutes later he roared into the compound on his machine. Onc more, he had to be carried from the motorbike to his seat an resumed drinking, a hero. Patrice, the chair and I went off t listen to some Dowayos who were happily singing a song abou adultery outside. Graciously, he offered me the chair. The joyfu singing was soon disrupted by a prison guard who had decided t record the music on his tape-recorder. I was aghast at thei treatment of him when he omitted to offer them a small sum fo the recording. The men set upon him with a will – still singing – th women trod on his machine; little boys bit his legs and seemed t be trying to insert sticks into his ears. Patrice was alarmed for hi chair; I was concerned that my own behaviour on so many occas ions had so closely resembled the guard's. I resolved to have word with Zuuldibo the next day and establish what it was tha had preserved me from similar treatment. It is never wise to b the witness to a crime in West Africa; police method consist largely of gathering witnesses, friends of the aggressed, etc., an beating them until one confesses. It is surprisingly effective Patrice and the chair and I moved on.

We returned to the *sous-préfet*'s party, now taken over entirel by the police, who were dancing with each other. After one rather coy dance with a sergeant I felt it was time to leave, and crept back to the mission at about five in the morning to be greeted by a chuckling Jon who refused to believe anything but the worst of my nocturnal activities.

Having now more or less finished up all serious research, it was time to deal with practicalities. I had been told that leaving the country was a rather more testing operation than reaching the airport with a valid ticket. It seemed I needed a permit to leave; until I had it, I was a prisoner in the country. This filled me with a sense of outrage. The precise moves to be made had been explained at the mission. Once again, it seemed incredible that any administrative process so cumbersome and pointless could ever be taken seriously; I was to learn otherwise.

The first shot of the campaign was fired in N'gaoundere. It was an unfortunate coincidence that I wished to apply for a visa to leave at the same time as my visa to stay expired. No one at the government office could be made to understand why I wanted both at the same time: either I was staying or I was going. I knew from experience that to be found without a valid visa during one of the numerous identity checks that punctuate any journey can be a time-consuming and expensive business. I should return in three days.

The next step was the tax office. Here too there were problems. It was unclear whether I should have gone to the one in N'gaoundere; my research permit had been issued in the capital, Yaounde. The area where I had worked was in the North and therefore administered through Garoua, but my last residence visa had come from N'gaoundere. They would have to consider the matter. I had to fill out a tax form containing the question 'Number of children. Are any still alive?' – a sad reflection of rates of infant mortality. I spent several days hanging around the office trying to see the inspector. Finally, I gained admittance. He agreed to deal with my case. The fact that I had paid British income tax all year was another major stumbling block. Was there a tax agreement between Cameroon and England? he asked. I confessed my ignorance. He closed my file with finality. Very well, I should have to bring a letter from my Embassy explaining the law on taxation. I very much doubted whether the Embassy could be cajoled into making any such declaration; moreover, I had no desire to go to Yaounde so we pushed arguments back and forth. He was adamant.

I hung around for another few days, hoping my residence visa might have come through. At the end of that time, I was told the radio was broken; it had been broken for a month. There was no possibility of a visa without talking to the capital.

I spent the next month oscillating between Garoua, N'gaoundere and Yaounde at huge cost to my finances and constitution. At the end of that time it was clear to me that there was no way I could ever legally get out of the country, being split as I was between three administrative areas. I discussed the matter with my French friends in Yaounde. Being of French nationality, they were much less troubled by these matters and could travel more or less as they pleased with a simple identity card. They put me in touch with a documentation expert from the French paymaster's office who gravely listened to my complex ills. There was no problem, he explained smilingly; I should adopt the standard ploy they all used. My story would be that I had lived all the time in the capital. I would need an address; I should borrow my friends'. Since I was white, I would need servants. Since I had servants I would need documents proving I paid them at least the government minimum salary and social security contributions. I should also borrow these from my friends. My story would be that we all shared a flat together and had put all the documents in the name of a single person for simplicity's sake; this would explain why my name did not appear on any document. This technique, it seemed, was regularly employed by all sorts of organizations to side-step the horrendous complexity of the bureaucracy. The only danger was that they would insist on visiting my domicile. This was not a great risk but the servants should be bribed and told what to say.

The plan was put into operation. Slowly, over the next few weeks, I crawled round the circuit collecting the nine necessary pieces of paper with stamps on. This involved much of the same treatment that I had endured when I first arrived; it no longer surprised or bothered me much.

My borrowed documents worked splendidly. The Inspector of Social Security did indeed decide to pay me a visit, but swiftly abandoned the idea when he learned that I had no car to drive him to my address. It was the rainy season; he refused to walk anywhere. I collected my stamps and plodded on.

Finally, I arrived at police headquarters where visas were actually given out. As usual, the day began with me being sent from one office to another as if no one had ever heard of the idea of giving out visas. I started at nine in the morning. By three in the afternoon I had got as far as the office of the chief of police. Only he could decide what to do since I was now in the position of having neither a visa to stay nor one to go. He listened to my tale with bored superiority. 'Give him a visa!' he snapped to a subordinate. No one asked to see the documents I had so painfully collected over seven weeks at such huge cost and involving a cast of dozens. I staggered from the office, weak with incredulity. So Moses must have felt when God handed him the tablets.

I began a phased withdrawal from Poli, relying once again on missionary aid to haul my kit to N'gaoundere, where my Laocoön-like wrestlings with bureaucracy had by now become a standing joke.

After the *sous-préfet*'s party I had decided, largely at the urging of Matthieu, to hold my own farewell party in the village. To this end, some forty bottles of beer had been obtained by devious means and Mariyo had agreed to brew a quantity of millet beer. This, of course, became a major problem in true Dowayo fashion. The money for the millet had gone to a man whose brother felt Zuuldibo owed him a cow. This man had taken it, but his brother was owed millet by his wife's parents who would get it from the woman's uncle, etc. The upshot of it all was that it was only at the very last minute that the millet was brought and the beer made. For two days the village was buzzing with excitement. Zuuldibo wove mats for the guests to sit on. Mariyo could be heard singing grinding songs as she crushed the millet. Children ran hither and thither borrowing calabashes and jars and generally getting under everyone's feet. They were especially keen to snap up anything I threw away. Aerosol spray cans were transmuted into musical instruments, matchboxes became

179

receptacles for secret objects in granaries, the label being carefully peeled off to serve as cigarette paper. Empty tins were highly sought after as cooking vessels. I had to take surplus medications out into the bush and bury them to stop children raking through them and eating them. Men kept dropping by just to look at the beer and spread the word.

All in all, the party was a wild success. Matthieu was annoyed that I refused to make a speech as the *sous-préfet* had, but gloried in being entrusted with the distribution of the beer. He made everyone line up and commanded his assistant in this enterprise to hand each person from the village a bottle of beer and informed them precisely who was giving it to them and why. I seemed the only one embarrassed at this proceeding. Soon the whole village was riotously drunk. Musical instruments appeared, one old man began shuffling his feet, another picked up the rhythm. A dance rapidly developed. Night fell, people still kept turning up from the fields, but miraculously the supplies held out. Two of the Chief's wives crouched at my feet and began to weep; the drummer knelt before me and pounded out an ever more insistent beat in the flickering firelight; the dancers circled, clapping their hands and stamping. It seemed to me that some response was being called for. It was clearly impossible to make a speech; I could not move for the press of the throng, so joining in the dance was out of the question. Miraculously, Matthieu appeared behind me with a handful of hundred-franc coins. 'Press a coin on each forehead, *patron*!' he hissed. I did as I was bid. Getting rather into the mood, I intoned a blessing, 'May your forehead be lumpy' – a sign of good fortune.

It seemed that this was exactly what was required. The Dowayos were delighted at this traditional benediction and danced away to attack the rest of the beer.

Matthieu and I retired to the hut where Zuuldibo and other worthies were assembled, and I finally ended up stumbling through a little speech of thanks and farewell; we then had to sit drinking for several hours although I desperately wanted the hard solitude of my bed. It amused me to note that in my service Matthieu had switched from total abstinence to being a considerable drinker, whereas I had been rendered virtually teetotal through hepatitis. Outside, the party continued to rage unabated; inside, we all fell into silence and listened to the music. One by one they crept off. Soon I was alone and tumbled gratefully into the bed. It began to rain. The roof began leaking again.

The next day I heard out of the blue that the car I had so successfully put out of my mind was 'almost repaired'. Investigation revealed that progress had indeed been made. It stood on four wheels, albeit with a rather raffish lean to one side. Actually getting it as far as my village took three attempts. Twice the engine seized up. The third time it burst into flames as I turned on the lights. All these, however, were relatively minor matters compared with actually laying hold of petrol, which I finally bought from an employee of the *sous-préfet*'s garage through the mediation of Augustin. Where he obtained it I pointedly refrained from asking.

All was ready for departure. Once I had started the car it was wiser not to stop it, given the state of the starter. A small group had turned out to see me off. Dowayos smiled vaguely and shuffled their feet, Barney the dog wagged his tail, Jon and Jeannie tried not to laugh as they assessed my chances of reaching N'gaoundere. A wave, a crunch of gears and I drove away from the mountains where I had spent so many months in so odd a pursuit. Every parting leaves an empty feeling, a slight touch of cosmic loneliness. It is hard not to begin at once forgetting that fieldwork consists largely of intense boredom, loneliness and mental and physical disintegration. A golden haze descends, the savages become more noble, the ritual more stirring, the past is restructured as leading inexorably to some great purpose of the present. It is only by reference to the diary I kept that I now know that my feeling was primarily one of hysterical joy to be done with Dowayoland.

The trip was not quite over, of course. The car, for example, had acquired a new feature in that it now sucked all rainwater channelled by the bodywork into air-ducts and sprayed it over the passengers. But I did make it as far as N'gaoundere where I devoted the next two weeks to attempting to ship out a trunk of pots. I was now quite prepared to see this treated as a major affront to Cameroonian national pride and an affair necessitating the direct intervention of seven different sets of officials.

There came the day, however, when I waved farewell to my friends from the mission, without whom my work could simply not have been done, and was asked for a final 'loan' by Matthieu before climbing into the plane.

The Cameroons had a last card to play. I was obliged to spend the night in the port of Duala where eating a single meal was enough to give me a riotous attack of the vomiting and diarrhoea for which that town is famed. My only comfort was that at least I had both a lavatory and bidet, so that I could escape that agonizing choice imposed by an English bathroom. The next morning I had to be virtually carried to the plane.

13　An English Alien

Most air journeys are nasty, brutish and long. The final stage of my fieldwork was made even more so by the fact that I was obliged to sit bolt upright, sipping like a maiden aunt from a bottle of Vichy water, all attention focused on my heaving stomach while something like a French 'Carry On' film was played at high volume for my delectation. The Sahara slipped away below.

It was at this point that I had the bright idea of stopping over in Rome where I had to change planes. I had a beatific vision of a quiet, cool room with fresh, slightly starched sheets. The shade of a leafy tree would fall on the bed; there might well be a calming fountain.

Once on the ground, I found that I could no longer carry my luggage and was obliged to deposit it in the left-luggage office. I watched my precious field notes and camera disappear into its gaping maw with a sceptical disbelief in their reappearance and in my lunacy at parting with them. Gripped firmly in my hand was my somewhat travel-soiled wardrobe. The trousers given me by my local missionary's wife attracted the curious stares of the elegant Romans. My wild-eyed and haggard look led *carabinieri* to follow me with their gaze.

I found my room. It was hot and noisy; all the lights buzzed; the price was obscene. This seemed about the right relationship between the desired and the attained. I settled down to sleep.

One of the least appreciated differences between an African village and a European city is in the passage of time. To one used to the regular pulse of farming life, where one thinks in seasons and the days have no names, urban dwellers seem to flash past in a frenzy of frustrated endeavour. I paced the streets of Rome like a Dowayo sorcerer whose unearthly slowness sets off his ritual role from everyday activities. Café menus offered so many possibilities that I felt unable to cope: the absence of choice in Dowayoland had led to a total inability to make decisions. In the field, I had dreamed endlessly of orgiastic eating; now I lived on ham sandwiches.

Having been warned repeatedly that I would quite inevitably be robbed, beaten and looted on the streets, I had been at pains to have only enough money on me to cover the cost of ham sandwiches. Perhaps it was no surprise to find on returning to my buzzing hotel room that the door had been levered from its hinges and all my possessions carried off: air-ticket, passport, money, even the remnants of my Dowayo wardrobe had vanished without trace. The management were adamant about their lack of responsibility. My West African abilities to rage and scream were greatly admired but left the situation unchanged. A quick survey of the one intact pocket in my outfit revealed that I had about a pound in the world. In such circumstances, the next move is quite obvious. I went to a café and, dispensing with ham sandwiches, ordered a beer and reflected on my plight. The proprietor was huge and quizzical. He established my nationality, my occupation, my marital status. He showed me a well-thumbed photograph of his large and much-loved brood. He had, he revealed, been a prisoner of war in Wales. The girls there, he affirmed bashfully, had been very passionate. Soon I was telling him all.

'So,' he summed up in an odd Romano-Celtic accent, 'you have no money, no ticket, no identification.' I agreed. 'Then I lend you ten thousand lire.' He slapped some notes on the bar. I ordered a ham sandwich. In my bemused state, such incredible generosity seemed no more unreasonable than the disaster that preceded it. I was back in fieldwork gear.

My benefactor rang the British Embassy while I demurred at further involvement with such persons, picturing an endless tour of Rome in search of stamped documents that would be plucked from my grasp by *ragazzi* before I could attain the plane. It was all arranged. First, I must go to the police to make a statement, then the Embassy would arrange for me to be repatriated. The very word seemed to imply shipment home in chains.

At the police station were assembled a vast horde of outraged, despairing and desolate tourists of all nationalities who had, it seemed, suffered the harsh attentions of Roman youth. The British, for some reason, were patiently sorted by a bored and indifferent policeman and placed in the same room as the Germans. The French were assigned, we noted with rage, a room that was both larger and cooler. A man with a strong Bradford accent addressed us all. 'It were Beryl I felt sorry for,' he announced. 'That's my wife.' He indicated a demure matron in tweed. 'She couldn't leave the camp site but they thought she were on the game. Men coming up to her, honking their horns. She had to throw plums at one bloke.' We regarded her speculatively. 'Then these two young fellers come up behind us on their motorbike, broke the window of the car at the back with a hammer and carried off us luggage like we wasn't there.'

The Germans demanded a translation, thinking that some important secret was being kept from them. I attempted to explain but had to give up since they seemed to be a group from a part of the Tyrol where there were no vowels.

Glutted on ham sandwiches, I sank back into fieldwork gear. At length I was led to an office deep underground and interviewed by a policeman. 'You were robbed at the railway station?' 'No, my hotel.' He grunted and made a note. 'What you lose?' I listed my possessions. 'How much cash?' 'About £100.' He shambled off.

Another officer appeared and, without explanation, deposited a wild-eyed, implausibly hirsute man in chains in the chair across from mine and departed. The man leaned forward and fixed me with a crazed stare. We both knew that the moment I looked away he would be at my throat. He stared at me. I stared back. Neither spoke. After an eternity my policeman reappeared, ignored the hirsute manaclee and handed me a statement to sign. The elegant Italian was not hard to comprehend. It declared roundly that I had been robbed of £1000 at the railway station. Feeling that I had been schooled to sterner stuff than this, I blithely signed.

I was now ready to assault the Embassy. Here again was a band of ravaged tourists attended by a stern and tight-lipped female consular officer. She was lecturing a very young and dirty girl in torn jeans. 'This is the third time you have been robbed at the railway station. We cannot keep on giving you passports. I shall telephone your parents.' The debauched waif sniffed. 'They don't care do they?' The consular officer compressed her lips in prim disapproval. 'Who was it this time?' 'Well we met these two boys . . .' The disapproving lady cut her off with a wave of the hand. 'I am bound to phone your parents. Wait here.' She departed, leaving us all feeling a mixture of sympathy, embarrassment and curiosity. The girl eyed us defiantly. The man ahead of me said something to her and she laughed. They went and sat down on a seat by the window while I dropped yet again into suspended animation.

Eventually the prim officer returned. 'Come here. I have agreed with your parents to advance you the fare back to England but I cannot permit you to remain here any longer. You will leave tomorrow.'

We all tensed, sensing that this was no blushing violet who would passively take such treatment. To our amazement, she smiled sweetly. 'That's all right, luv. This bloke' – she indicated the man who had been speaking to her – 'has invited me to stay on his yacht.' Together they swept out to our thunderous, though silent, applause.

My own processing was more routine. With hardly more than a glance of distaste at my trousers and a pout of disapproval, my passage was arranged. I took the precaution of adjusting my version of events to fit that contained in the statement.

So it was that eighteen months after my departure I arrived back in England, possessing a pair of torn trousers, seven smeared and stained exercise books of notes on West Africa, a camera clogged with sand and a statement in Italian. I had lost forty pounds and was scorched a dark brown, and acquired vivid yellow eyeballs. I confronted the immigration officer.

'Passport?'

'I'm afraid I've lost my passport.' I handed him my statement in Italian. He narrowed his eyes. 'You *are* English, sir?'

'Oh . . . ah . . . yes.'

'You would be prepared to sign a statement to that effect, sir?'

'Certainly.'

'All right. On your way.' He waved me through.

It couldn't be that easy. I suspected a trap. I looked cunning. 'You mean I don't have to shout, threaten you or offer you money?'

'On your way, sir.'

A paradox that has much exercised mathematicians is that of the Einsteinian space traveller. Having journeyed at great speed for several months around the universe, he returns to Earth to find that whole decades have passed. The anthropological traveller is in the reverse position. He goes away for what seems an inordinately long period to other worlds, ponders cosmic problems, ages greatly. When he returns, only a few months have elapsed. The acorn he planted has not become a great tree; it has scarcely had time to put forth a tentative shoot. His children have not grown to adulthood; only his closest friends have noticed he has been away at all.

It is positively insulting how well the world functions without one. While the traveller has been away questioning his most basic assumptions, life has continued sweetly unruffled. Friends continue to collect matching French saucepans. The acacia at the foot of the lawn continues to come along nicely.

The returning anthropologist does not expect a hero's welcome but the casualness of some friends seems excessive. An hour after my arrival, I was phoned by one friend who merely remarked tersely. 'Look, I don't know where you've been but you left a pullover at my place nearly two years ago. When are you coming to collect it?' In vain one feels that such questions are beneath the concern of a returning prophet.

A strange alienness grips you, not because anything has changed but rather because you no longer see things as 'natural' or 'normal'. 'Being English' seems as much a pose as 'being Dowayo'. You find yourself discussing the things that seem important to your friends with the same detached seriousness that you used to discuss witchcraft with your villagers. The result of this lack of fit is a brooding sense of insecurity only heightened by the vast numbers of rushing white people you meet everywhere.

Anything connected with shopping seems inordinately difficult.

The sight of the shelves of a supermarket groaning with super-abundance of food induces either nauseous revulsion or helpless dithering. I would either go three times round the store and give up the attempt to decide, or buy vast quantities of the most luxurious goods and whimper with the terror that they would be snatched from me.

After months of isolation, polite conversation is extraordinarily hard. Long silences are taken as brooding displeasure while people in the street react quite badly to the sight of a man quite openly talking to himself. Adjusting to the rules of interaction also poses problems. When the milkman left unordered milk on the step one day my reaction was to race after him shouting and raging after the West African fashion. I believe I may even have seized him by the collar. The poor man was greatly discountenanced. By West African rules I was merely being firm, by English rules an insufferable lout. Seeing oneself suddenly in this light can be a humbling experience.

Some small things give enormous satisfaction. I became addicted to cream cakes; a friend conceived a hopeless passion for strawberries. Running water and electric light were frankly incredible. At the same time, I developed odd quirks. It troubled me to throw away empty bottles or paper bags; in Africa they were so valuable. The finest moment of the day was waking up with a start and feeling a warm flood of relief to be no longer in Africa. My notebooks lay neglected on the desk; I felt a deep revulsion to even touching them which lasted for months.

One of the strangest psychological experiences was the arrival of the trunk of pots that I had dispatched what seemed like months before. I had wrapped them carefully in Dowayo cloth and packed them in a metal cabin trunk plastered with stickers declaring the fragility of the contents in four languages. Zuuldibo had been appalled at such meanness. Why did I not give them to the villagers? It was known that I was quite rich enough, like the woman who made the pots themselves, to buy gaudy enamelware from Nigeria. My wives would surely not be pleased when I handed them pottery from a village.

It was strange to see the trunk that had once stood in my hut lying in a dank, cold shed in London. Its shape had been completely transformed. On dispatch it had been rectangular; now it was almost wholly spherical. Large boot marks on the lid attested to the agent that had worked this wonder. I had to prise off the lid with a tyre lever. It is always odd to receive a package from oneself: it smacks of split personality, especially when the person who sent it is so rapidly becoming alien to him who receives it. My friends without exception admired the elegant simplicity of the pots. What a pity I had spoiled them by using them; could I not have bought some cheap imported pans and saved these as too beautiful to use? It would have been nice to introduce them to Zuuldibo and let them fight it out. The returned fieldworker accepts both positions, identifies with neither.

It is impossible, of course, at such moments not to try to draw up a balance sheet of profit and loss. I had certainly learnt a lot about a small and relatively unimportant people of West Africa. Finishing fieldwork is always a matter of definition, not of fact. It would have been quite possible to go on for another five years in Dowayoland, albeit with diminishing returns, without exhausting the scope of a project aimed at 'understanding' a people so different from ourselves. But more general competences always lie beneath the particular. Henceforth I was to find that the monographs of which anthropology as a subject is composed would appear to me in quite different light. I would be able to feel which passages were deliberately vague, evasive, forced, where data were inadequate or irrelevant in a way that had been impossible before Dowayoland. All this makes the work of other anthropologists more available than it had ever been before. I also felt that in attempting to understand the Dowayo view of the world I had tested the relevance of certain very general models of interpretation and cultural symbolism. On the whole they had stood up pretty well and I felt much happier about their place in the scheme of things.

Purely personally, there had also been great changes. In common with many other fieldworkers, my health had been shattered for some time to come. My vague liberal faith in the ultimate cultural and economic salvation of the Third World had received a sharp knock. It is a common trait of returned fieldworkers, as they stumble around their own culture with the clumsiness of returned astronauts, to be simply uncritically grateful to be a Westerner, living in a culture that seems suddenly very precious and vulnerable; I was no exception. But there is something insidiously habit-forming in anthropological fieldwork. The ethnographic hangover is no more effective as aversion therapy than any other. Several weeks after my return I phoned the friend whose conversation had sent me to the field in the first place.

'Ah, you're back.'

'Yes.'

'Was it boring?'

'Yes.'

'Did you get very sick?'

'Yes.'

'Did you bring back notes you can't make head or tail of and forget to ask all the important questions?'

'Yes.'

'When are you going back?'

I laughed feebly. Yet six months later I returned to Dowayoland.

FOR THE BEST IN PAPERBACKS, LOOK FOR THE 🐧

In every corner of the world, on every subject under the sun, Penguin represents quality and variety – the very best in publishing today.

For complete information about books available from Penguin – including Puffins, Penguin Classics and Arkana – and how to order them, write to us at the appropriate address below. Please note that for copyright reasons the selection of books varies from country to country.

In the United Kingdom: Please write to *Dept E.P., Penguin Books Ltd, Harmondsworth, Middlesex, UB7 0DA.*

If you have any difficulty in obtaining a title, please send your order with the correct money, plus ten per cent for postage and packaging, to *PO Box No 11, West Drayton, Middlesex*

In the United States: Please write to *Dept BA, Penguin, 299 Murray Hill Parkway, East Rutherford, New Jersey 07073*

In Canada: Please write to *Penguin Books Canada Ltd, 2801 John Street, Markham, Ontario L3R 1B4*

In Australia: Please write to the *Marketing Department, Penguin Books Australia Ltd, P.O. Box 257, Ringwood, Victoria 3134*

In New Zealand: Please write to the *Marketing Department, Penguin Books (NZ) Ltd, Private Bag, Takapuna, Auckland 9*

In India: Please write to *Penguin Overseas Ltd, 706 Eros Apartments, 56 Nehru Place, New Delhi, 110019*

In the Netherlands: Please write to *Penguin Books Netherlands B.V., Postbus 195, NL–1380AD Weesp*

In West Germany: Please write to *Penguin Books Ltd, Friedrichstrasse 10–12, D–6000 Frankfurt/Main 1*

In Spain: Please write to *Alhambra Longman S.A., Fernandez de la Hoz 9, E–28010 Madrid*

In Italy: Please write to *Penguin Italia s.r.l., Via Como 4, I-20096 Pioltello (Milano)*

In France: Please write to *Penguin Books Ltd, 39 Rue de Montmorency, F-75003 Paris*

In Japan: Please write to *Longman Penguin Japan Co Ltd, Yamaguchi Building, 2–12–9 Kanda Jimbocho, Chiyoda-Ku, Tokyo 101*

Native Land

Nigel Barley, famous for his field work in Cameroon and Indonesia, turns the quizzical eye of a 'professional alien' on the culture and people of his native land.

With tremendous wit and perception he opens our eyes to the *données* of English life: the ritual, tradition and ceremony inherent in every aspect of our day-to-day existence. Drawing comparisons with primitive cultures, he asks such questions as what is the symbolism of the wedding cake? What is the significance of the layout of rooms in the average English semi-detached? In what ways does a rural community differ from an urban one? How do we express our patriotism or our belief in God?

Aided in his research by 'insider' Jim Bachelor, Nigel Barley discovers that the clichés about the English no longer hold true. Yet despite the disparate nature of our lives and our frequently bizarre and eccentric behaviour, the essence of true Englishness is still discernible.

A Plague of Caterpillars

The chance to witness a rare circumcision ceremony was an opportunity not to be missed.

Nigel Barley's return to Cameroon promised much. The Dowayos, a pagan mountain tribe, were due to perform their fearsome ancient ritual for the first time in six or seven years.

Armed with Christmas pudding and Cheddar cheese, Dr Barley embarked on his quest to witness this unusual anthropological phenomenon, only to find his way strewn with difficulties – not least an extraordinary plague of black, hairy caterpillars.

The author of *The Innocent Anthropologist* has again produced a catalogue of hilarious anecdotes, as well as a skilful reflection on the problems of different cultures understanding one another.